BOOKS BY RONA|

Jesus the Lost Years - The C

Paranormal explained - Synchronicities

Alien Monk 2012 - Skulls of the Apocalypse

Alien Monk 2013 - Armageddon is coming

Alien Monk - Aliens on the moon

Alien Monk - Spirit of Nostradamus

Alien Monk 2

The voyages of Joseph of Avalon

Jesus in Cornwall - The Secret Knowledge

Joseph Escapes to Glastonbury

The Clintons and the Glastonbury Connection

First Alien Contact - Aliens sex by numbers

Alien and the Paranormal - Interdimentional reality

With great pleasure from;

Ronald Rayner

26 Dec. 2023

COPYRIGHT

Distributors
Amazon Books and Amazon Kindle
Manager to the Author, Maddison Mears,

Add Design
Telephone (UK) 0845 643 6395 Email: info@add-design.co.uk

ISBN Number: 9780957393967

Publisher
Blackthorn Publishing Ltd, Third Floor, 207 Regent St, London W1B 3HH United Kingdom

Printer: Blackwater Sign & Print, 19e Spital Road, Maldon, Essex CM9 6DY
Telephone: 01621 858416 www.blackwatersignandprint.co.uk

INDEX

INTRODUCTION

List of Drawings and Photographs

INTRODUCTION

ARE VISIONARIES BORN OR MADE? A DEFINITIVE ANSWER BY THE WORLD-LEADING MYSTIC RONALD RAYNER.

Evolution is evolving, New Men, New Women, with fully evolved super-conscious awareness, who eat technology for breakfast, are coming.

HOW THE 'ONLINE GURU' IS CHANGING THE WORLD

The biggest breakthrough since Einstein, the Rayner
theory of the Paranormal is explained.

I started researching and writing about mysticism in the 1960s, and over the last six decades enthusiasts and followers of the phenomenon in several countries have grown to describe me, personally, as the world's greatest Mystic and Prophet. I am very flattered of course, but now I feel obligated to describe my childhood, to the point at which my mother revealed to me at the age of eleven years old that I had inherited her gift. However, with hindsight, I question the word gift, because from my own personal experience, I don't really know whether it's a gift or a curse: seeing painful events that I would have preferred not to have seen in advance. Furthermore, there are no rewards for predicting earthquakes in advance of the event, as I predicted for Iceland, three months in advance, being proven in one of my books. Ridicule, but no apologies after being proven correct. I have suffered as being regarded as weird or strange for many years, a consequence of which friends can be counted on one hand. Writing is a lonely business, more particularly when people one thinks of as friends let one down. Fortunately, the sad days are offset by intelligent and creative enthusiasts of my work, by those who love my work, particularly when I was able to prove through research that most women are gifted with Clairvoyance, to the annoyance of their husbands, all of which culminated in my discovering the Paranormal as a reality – 'The Rayner Theory of the Paranormal', which, over time, will change thinking by scientists across the planet. I loved my mother more than words can describe. She was always correct. Before her death, she told me that God would speak to me, and it happened. The most wondrous moments in my life, brought back the feeling when, whilst filming in the Holy Sepulchre in Jerusalem, Sister Katarina who tended the three main Altars gave me a piece of Calvary with the blessing that I would be able to read the 'Urim and Thummim'.

In the beginning, came BIG BANG, creating every element and particle with its own inbuilt mathematic structure, like the seed from a flower, or tree, containing within it the complete code that instructs seeds to grow and develop to fruition, and continue to evolve, but scientists have not yet grasped this vital fact. Acceptance of this will spur scientists on to finish the work by Einstein and Darwin who did not have the technology that is available to science today to change the world view of evolution into future time

Along with BIG Bang, there evolved the Paranormal, a shadow Earth: Invisible, Instantaneous, where Time just is. Where mystical, but very real invisible forces exist, proven clearly by Synchronicities. Another phenomenon completely missed by scientists to this present day.

In recent times, one piece of continuous evolution has fetched a big change to religious worship, as a direct result of the use of computers, and iPhones. These enable anyone to be an online GURU, across the internet, creative people who have grown large numbers of followers, largely taking over the roles that were the preserve of Ministers of a Church. This is one of the many reasons church-going has fallen to below one percent of a nearly seventy million population in the United Kingdom, an inconvenient fact ignored by church leaders, as is moving to more sensible sermons, for example: 'In the past we taught that God created the world in six days, this was of course before scientists proved that our God is mightier than we thought. Our God has given everything a purpose; planet Earth is billions of years old, and there are around 400,000 Galaxies in our universe. Humankind came down from several variations of early humans, and so on". Real scientific facts that church-goes can believe. Will the church ever change its sermons or teach that the path for prayer or repentance will go direct to God, instantaneously, through the forces of the Paranormal. The development of the on-line Guru spells out a real danger to the future for organised religions, that will fetch changes across the world.

Perhaps the biggest development is 'Wellness guru'. Many claim that if you feel burnt out, unwell, tired all the time: Buy our pills, eat the foods we eat, subscribe to our podcast, and you will be cured of your ailments. It appears obvious that many followers have lost weight or grown healthier. These efforts by 'Guru', assuming that their claims are not untrue, must go a long way to helping people who find it near impossible to get a doctor's appointment, or have to wait at least twelve hours in A and E.

This book is the first in the world to explain the truth and fact that UFOs are an Interdimensional reality that scientists do not yet understand. This book explains this reality.

UFO's ARE AN INTERDIMENTIONAL REALITY

We are on the cusp of the development of evolved new men and new women. Those who live by every technological idea and gadget, eat technology for breakfast, meditate, follow Wellness Guru; have developed super conscious awareness, and left normal men and women behind. They are coming, but will you be one of those left behind?

This book also compares how alien enthusiasts over half a century ago connected briefly with an alien phenomenon using Ouija Boards, and compares these results achieved by a dedicated select group of modern mediums devoted entirely to contacting and speaking with aliens, plus 'Men in Black'.

A NEW REVELATION
STOP BLAMING GOD

I pondered for many years; why I, Ronald Rayner, was singularly chosen when I was filming my Documentary 'Jerusalem' in the Holy Sepulchre, Jerusalem, to be given a piece of Calvary, by Sister Katarina (who was attending the three main Altars) that came away into Sister's hand from the spot where the 'Cross of Crucifixion' went into the rock of Calvary, sited in the Holy Sepulchre, Jerusalem, whilst she was cleaning the entry area before an attractive reinforced plate was fitted. The answer came to me many years later in the form of a Revelation, or Epiphany, during the night of Saturday, 18th February, 2023.

THE REVELATION OR EPIHPHANY

Planet Earth is an active planet in our solar system, held into position by a moon, the degree of which varies over a small range over time. Our planet is an active planet because it has Plate Tectonics that are constantly on the move, either colliding, pulling apart or one moving above another. Movements that can cause Earthquakes of varying intensity. All of which has NOTHING WHAT-SO-EVER TO DO WITH GOD, The Evolutionary Powers of our planet. Neither can God change or stop the natural activity of Plate Tectonics on planet Earth because our planet behaves according to the laws governing our solar system. Understand this; if humankind has built dwellings etc and are themselves in the area where an earthquake take place – their property may be destroyed and they themselves may be killed. Again, nothing what-so-ever to do with God, nor can God stop the Earthquake happening, SO STOP BLAMING GOD FOR THE DESTRUCTION CAUSED BY EARTHQUAKES OR VOLCANIC ERUPTIONS! The evolution of the Solar system, and the Suns, Planets, Galaxies, and so on do their own thing, and are nothing to do with the God.

Chapter 1

ARE VISIONARIES AND MYSTICS BORN OR MADE?
About author Ronald Rayner

Seeds of Mysticism

My earliest recollections of my mother are walking hand in hand with her across grass fields to school. I remember a siren sounding, and looking up as the noise of German bombers appeared in the sky. Soon to be confirmed by an 'air raid' warning, followed by a different tone of siren for the 'all clear', after the bombers had dropped their bombs and headed back to Germany. Mother remained completely unperturbed I recall being excited by the prospect of my first day at school, but excitement soon gave way to bewilderment when I found myself sitting with children who were happy playing with sand and coloured bricks. I was also disappointed after being told by my mother that the teacher knew everything, to discover that she did not know my name, but had to ask. Spotting an open window at the other end of the classroom, I satisfied my frustration by climbing from the window and running home about a mile across the grass fields.

My freedom soon turned to alarm when I discovered that no one was home, and the stark realisation that I was locked out. A realisation that really struck home when the air raid warning sounded. I felt a little scared at first, and took shelter in a bin store at the side of our very large house. I looked out from behind the bins and heard the sound of guns firing in the distance. I plucked up courage to climb onto the roof of the bin store to see what was happening. On the distant railway embankment, a large gun on a flatbed carriage behind a railway engine was firing at German bombers, I forgot my fear with the excitement of seeing fighter planes with red white and blue circles on their wings chasing after the bombers, and the gun turrets at the front and rear of the German bombers returning fire.

I was engrossed in what was happening in the skies when a Wolsey car screeched to a halt outside the house. It was mother. She rushed from the car and ordered me to get down from the bin shed, and follow her into the house. We both sat in silence holding hands in a cupboard under the main stairs. Mothers look informed me that men are never afraid and have a stiff upper lip. I could smell Port on her breath, and spotted a packet of jellied eels in the pocket of her hacking jacket. We both sat silently until the 'all clear' siren sounded. Only then did mother realise that I should be at school. "Why are you at home," she asked; with an air of surprise. "The School Board Inspector could be here any minute. What excuse am I going to make to the Inspector. Do you want me to go to prison for keeping you at home when you should be attending class." "I am sorry mother, it just seemed silly staying there when I was not being taught anything by the teacher." "You, Ronald, are returning to school tomorrow morning. You will apologise to the teacher, and promise that you will not run away again." Tea was two meagre slices of bread and jam, and a cup of cocoa. My mother explained that she had run out of Food Coupons, and that all she could buy on the black market was a loaf of bread, a pot of jam, and some sawdust sandwiches, as they were called, because of the fine sawdust mixed with the sausage meat. by the butcher. My treat was to be allowed to listen to BBC radio until 7pm when I was off to bed.

That night an air raid siren went off, but I could not hear my parents stirring. I rushed into their bedroom in which they slept in separate beds, shouting "air raid, air raid." They did not bother to get from their beds but ordered me into the cupboard under the main staircase. My mother calling out, "you are the future and must be saved". I fell asleep in the cupboard and laid there until next morning when my mother woke me, pulled me into the wash room to get ready for school.

That morning was surreal. Walking across the grass I spotted an oak tree covered with shiny things. They looked like fountain pens and toys. An air raid warden called out, "don't touch anything, they will explode in your hand and injure you." They were dropped in the night near schools by German bombers to injure children and damage morale.
As soon as I reached school we were marched into assembly and given a short lecture by a policeman about not touching potentially explosive devices. Before being dismissed into the playground. Returning to school assembly a boy with a shaved head from a 'flea inspection' was stood in front of the school and whipped six times with a long thin cane for stealing school milk, by passing it through the school railings to his family, who were gypsies. We were then dismissed again into the playground.

Whilst we were in the playground, we followed the daily routine of drinking our daily bottle of milk, watered down and tasteless, straight from the farm. I ran around to stretch my legs; had barely reached the railings with my arms out flying like a bird, when there was a screaming sound. A German Messerschmidt was machine-gunning the playground. Only one pass, and it screamed off into the distance. No one was hurt, but for a few scratches from scattered tarmac. We were ordered to lunch, when the school caretaker appeared with brooms and a shovel, calling out, "that was a stray that was, now get in to lunch, and allow me to get on with my job."

School dinners were fantastic. Probably the only square meal most children had in a day. Small tables with four chairs round and a sort of plastic table cloth; waited on by dinner ladies. I don't know how children would have survived during those years of food rationing without those school meals. Everyone appeared underweight, adults and children alike. Bad days were when a German bomb hit a water main in the district, and there was nothing to drink on a hot summer's day from the press and squirt, drinking tap. It was not unusual when I arrived home from school to stand in a queue with my mother carrying a couple of buckets, and waiting for a tanker to come round with water.

That evening my mother told me to take the pavement route to school, where I was more likely to find shelter in a doorway if the air raid siren sounded. As fate would have it, the next day walking along the pavement, I ignored the air raid warning, carried on walking to school when I found myself flying backwards surrounded by warm air; everything was quiet. I continued backwards, grazing the back of my legs on a dwarf wall, and landing on my back on grass. I was trying to make sense of things when I was grabbed by the back of my collar and pulled backwards into a hallway, continuing into a passage way, dragging along a loose rug under my legs over some linoleum. An elderly lady helped me up into an oak chair covered in a 'rexine', fabric. I was shaking like a leaf, and I was scared. She said "don't worry son, I'll make you a cup of sweet tea, and pop in something to get rid of the shakes." She poured the tea from a large dark brown clay teapot covered with a knitted tea cosy, in bright green. Then she carefully poured a teaspoon of whisky from a bottle into the tea. I must say the tea was the best I had ever tasted. The shakes went after a few minutes. She said, "I drink tea and whisky all the time during air raids because it stops me shaking". She gave me an apple and said I had better get along to school, but to call in and see her any time.

Along the road I saw two houses on fire, the explosion from which had blown me over the wall. I could hear the bells from fire engines on their way to the fire. I wanted to stop and watch, but I knew I would be in trouble with both my parents, and the school, if I did not attend. The School Board man would be on the doorstep of my home later that day demanding to know my whereabouts, and threatening to fine my parents if it happened again. I was too shaky to run to school so I walked as fast as I could, but not fast enough. When I arrived at the school gates, the playground was empty, and I knew I was in trouble. As I walked into the school a tall thin man who I recognised as the headmaster yelled at me to stop. Come here boy, and give me that apple. You know you are not allowed to fetch food into the school. Furthermore, you are late, and I am going to teach you not to be late again. He then smacked me very hard on the backs of my legs. I was small, thin and wiry. Back of my legs immediately became red and swollen. I could barely hobble to my classroom, or sit in the chair, when I was then reprimanded for fidgeting.

Arriving home my father, who was on three days leave from the Army, listened to my story and exploded with anger when he saw the swelling on the back of my legs. He climbed onto his horse and rode off towards the school. My father told me later that he arrived at school, tied his horse, and headed for the school gates when he spotted the headmaster who took off like the devil was after him. My father gave chase to the High Street, and caught the headmaster, just as he was mounting a bus. He dragged him off the bus and told him to put up his fists, because he was going to teach the headmaster a lesson about hitting tiny children. My father said the headmaster was really scared, apologised profusely, and promised it would not happen again. My father said he allowed him to go off after a friendly punch to the stomach.

Next morning my mother told me I should avoid walking to school on my own by knocking for a friend, and I decided to collect my friend Phillip on the way. I knocked on his front door, an old lady who was very pale answered. "Ronald," she said, then pulled me close to her, and went down on one knee, holding me by the shoulders and looking into my eyes. "I have some bad news. Phillip and his mother my daughter, were killed the other day by the bomb that went off close by. They were visiting her cousin on her birthday. I don't know what to say Ronald, except that they are both in Heaven together;" she started crying and slowly closed the door. I was shocked, and I ran off to school half crying. Entering the classroom, I went straight to the teacher, explained what had happen and begged to be seated elsewhere in the classroom. He answered, "I have 58 children in the class boy, and if you think for one minute that I am going to change the seating plan for you boy, you can think again. Get over it boy, there is a war on, and if you say another word, well, you know what will happen."

Next day I awoke. It was a Saturday. I felt very lonely, slightly afraid, and started to panic when the air raid warning sounded. My mother said she had noticed a change in me, and said that every morning I must tell her my dreams that previous night. My dreams were always in vivid technicolour. "I dreamed that I was on a train with my cousin Joyce. The air raid sounded. We needed to jump from the slam door compartment immediately because it was going to be hit by an incendiary device, and burst into flame."

Astonishingly, my mother announced that my cousin Joyce, who was older than me would be taking me by train to carry a present to an aunt whose birthday it was, and who had just lost her husband to the war effort. It was a great day, because it was good to be with someone who made a fuss of me, and not hurt me like the teachers at school. My aunt said goodbye and gave me a fruit cake, in a tin, to take home to mother. I dozed for most of the train journey, but just as it was getting dark the train shuddered to a stop. We peered from the carriage window and saw the engine covered in flames, probably from an incendiary bomb. I pulled my cousins arm, and told her we must jump from the train because our carriage was the next to be hit. It was quite a steep drop from the carriage to the track. We both managed the drop but the momentum sent us rolling down the embankment. I was wearing short trousers and my legs were becoming quite scratched, but I never let go of the precious cake. We ran straight ahead holding hands until noticing we were entering a pond. "Great," shouted my cousin, "I know where we are, we are heading home." We heard a loud bang. Looking round we saw that the carriage we had just left was in flames, true to my dream. The light from the flames helped us to see our way. As soon as we reached the grass flats, we parted company heading for our own homes with me hanging onto the fruit cake for dear life. There was a blackout, no lights, but my mother was hanging out from an upstairs window looking at the train on fire in the distance. I called out. She came rushing to the front door, "my son, my son, you are safe." She grabbed me calling, "I thank God that you are both safe." She soon recovered and asked what was in the tin. "A fruit cake mother, our favourite." " I'll make some acorn coffee for Ronald to enjoy with a slice of cake, then it's off to bed, and hopefully there will be no heavy gun firing keeping us awake tonight."

I woke up realising it was a Sunday; porridge oats and Tate and Lyle Golden Syrup, delicious. Sitting round the breakfast table my mother pushed her hands across the table holding my fingers. "Your dream Ronald, saved both you and your cousin Joyce," "but mother," I interceded, "who decides who is going to live and who is going to die? the passengers who did not jump from the carriages; some will have been burnt alive, was it because they were bad people?"

Mother said nothing but pulled me closer. "I am going to reveal to you Ronald something of importance that I want you to keep to yourself. You, like me, are going to grow up to be a Seer and Mystic. I know from listening to your many dreams that this is so, and that you have inherited these gifts from me. As young as you are in age Ronald, I want you to promise me now that you will never use your gifts to harm anyone. Instead, try to do something every day to make someone happy, kind words, a small gift; do harm to no one. Do these things faithfully Ronald, and this is how you show thanks to God for your gifts, and whilst you have these gifts, no harm will ever come to you."

"Another of your gifts will be the ability to scry, and astral travel. You will be able to look into a bowl of water or a crystal ball, and travel to another place, but more about that when you are older."

I was surprised at her words, and felt very curious about this aspect of my gifts. I asked my mother; if God would be happy about me travelling around spiritually? "Of course, Ronald," and reached over for her Bible.
"A Hebrew Mystic and Prophet in the Old Testament, EZEKIEL, prophesized the destruction of Jerusalem and Israel.

[Verse 14] Then the spirit lifted me up, and took me away, and I went in bitterness, in the heat of my Spirit; but the hand of the Lord was strong upon me.
[Verse 15] Then I came to them of the Captivity at Tel-a-bid by the river of Che-bar, and I sat where they sat, and remained there astonished amongst them seven days.

The ability to Astral travel, has always been available to God's chosen Ronald, as is the gift of Mysticism – to see into future time, and Prophesy. You will have the ability to reflect a Curse, but use this only when you are an adult, and only as a last resort. Now listen to me Ronald. If you reflect a curse and you are wrong, it will return to you sevenfold. We will discuss these matters when you grow older"

It was a glorious summer's day, with the bonus that there were no air raid warnings, as I walked with my mother in the woods to study the minnows in the ponds.

Just before darkness I asked where father was. "He's on Fire Watch at the school. Why not run along and see him and wish him goodnight?" I went into the school and up four flights of darkened stairs, then through a door onto the roof. There he was, wearing his tin helmet, singing and tap dancing on the wide capstones around the edge of the roof. He saw me, grabbed me up in his arms, and swung me round standing on the capstones, which was very scary. Standing on the tarred roof from behind the safety of the cap stones I looked ahead, the scene was surreal. Not the scene of victory which was the theme of the song father was singing. Houses in the distance were on fire. There was the clanging of fire bells and ambulances. In the sky fighter planes were chasing German bombers. There were Barrage Balloons around large buildings, and searchlights lighting up the night sky, pinpointing bombers for the guns below. It was a scene from a dream, a scene I shall never forget; my first glimpse of the communicated insanity of war. My father carried me down the flights of stairs, and on to home. I must have fallen sound asleep, because I do not remember anything until my mother was tucking me into my bed.

As a lay scientist I have always believed that factual, unbiased evidence is the only basis on which to judge the real world in which we live. Consequently, I have to ask myself, 'What If'? What if Mysticism is just imagination? After all, imagination is at the very heart of what it is to be human. Flashes of imagination by early man built the first fires, boats, tools, collaboration, music, the list is endless.

Was it imagination when the Prophet Moses began to wonder about the one God, the one Eternal Being, as opposed to the many gods the Hebrews had been worshipping? Was it the imagination of Moses that brought forth the Ten Commandments? was Moses the first greatest Mystic and Prophet? I personally have always been fascinated by the Prophet Moses, and have painted large oils depicting Moses with the two tablets of stone that contained the Commandments. Moses prophesied, that we are not alone and the belief that there is a better future with endless possibilities for everyone, if they follow the rules written in the Ten Commandments.

If you have any difficulty imagining who or what God is, God is the ultimate power and influence in the universe. How powerful? Imagine the great forces and power of Black Holes colliding at the centre of galaxies. The photographs of the massive systems where new stars, planets and galaxies are created. The smallest things such as Strings whose vibrations fetch atomic particles into existence. The transmission of all these vibrations and forces across the universe, then you have some idea of our God and the Spirit of transmission across the universe. The universe is constantly creating and expanding. One can see a plan for everything to continually evolve, including the creatures, including mankind. When evolution stops, and man retreats back to the animal from which he came, defeating the purpose in the universe, it is not difficult to see that he will be wiped away, like Sodom and Gomorrah, because he is not following the very purpose of the Power of the Universe. Anything that goes against the purpose of the universe will be wiped away by catastrophes. I have seen a glimpse!

Returning to my childhood, at breakfast father announced that he had been advised to take us every night to the nearest tube station, where we would be safe from the German bombs. I objected strongly because I had dreamed of a bomb dropping on the entrance of a tube station killing many people. That is the end of that Ronald, we will not be going near any Tube station. Sadly, a bomb did hit the entrance of a tube station killing hundreds, but for the sake of morale that story never reached the press or radio.

Whilst we were all comfortably round the table drinking tea, I asked my mother why I did not have a middle name like other children. "Unfortunately, Ronald, your Christening did not go to plan. The woman I employed as your Nanny, during the daytime, was not what she pretended to be. She was a bit of a drinker, and instead of taking you for a walk in the park, she used to park your pram in the back of a pub where the food was prepared, and sat herself in the bar. All the words that came out from pub workers were swear words, F… You. F… Off. You get the picture Ronald. It transpired that these words became part of your language, I had to delay your Christening hoping these words would go away after you no longer heard them. Come the Christening, you looked very pretty in blue with your long blond curls. The Minister eagerly grabbed you in his arms, pouring water on your forehead from a large spoon. Perhaps the water was cold because you became upset and shouted at the Minister "f… you f… you f… off… f… you", and you would not stop Ronald. The poor man was so startled he shoved you into my arms, and rushed off muttering "Terrible mother", and worse. Father chased him from the church to give him a smack and demanded an apology, but the Minister disappeared into the cemetery, and never returned, and that was the end of it…no Christening, and no middle name Ronald. However, this story, although true, must not be repeated at school, Ronald. Your father disliked the Minister because of the rumours that persisted about him interfering with young children, after Sunday school. With all the men at war, there was no one who would take him on, particularly after the Bishop had asked your father not to threaten the Minister. The Minister was obviously aware that father was not going to leave it at that, and moved on"

One morning, eating my porridge, my mother said that she barely recognised my father on his brief visits from the Army. I butted in; "father told me how many Germans he had killed in hand-to-hand fighting with his commando knife. He boasted how he drove over German bodies when beating a hasty retreat." "Yes, Ronald, father has changed beyond recognition. He seems very cold and unfeeling; even distant and violent. During his last visit the police brought him home from a pub where he beat up three Irishmen boasting about Hitler. The Police did not press charges. I suppose I am not really surprised Ronald after hearing about the constant deaths he witnesses, and has had to fight to the death with his knife when he ran out of ammunition. I have to tell you Ronald, at the moment father is lost at sea. The ship on which he was being transported to France was sunk in the Channel." Later that day my mother heard that father had been pulled from the sea after surviving for two days, and was in hospital.

Three weeks later I arrived home from school to find my father waiting for me in the front garden of the house. He whisked me off my feet, and said "I am here to protect you son. I hear you have been arriving home with swellings on your legs and face where you have been hit by your teachers. Tomorrow I will be meeting you from school, and may God help any teacher who has hit you so hard as to make your leg swell. I have killed more Germans with my knife than I can count on one hand." Then he took off his shirt and showed me the scars of knife wounds on his body. I finished off my bread and jam, and father whisked me off to bed.

Next day word must have spread around the school that my father was home. No teacher smacked me hard on the back of my legs or hit me round the head with a book.

Looking back at those nightmare days, I can understand why teachers were so tense. They never knew when they arrived home if their house would be still standing. Their pay was a mere £495 per annum, and well below average pay at that time. I have to say that the Teachers, Headmasters/Mistresses, who kept schools open during the Air Raids in World War Two, are definitely the unsung heroes of World War Two.

Writing the above extracts from my life, I have convinced myself that some natural Visionaries and Mystics, like myself are born, but those who follow meditation and the paranormal will evolve to become Seers and Mystics in their own right. I also believe a 'plaque' dedicated to the teachers who kept schools open during World-War Two should be placed in a prominent position at every teacher training college.

The Great Prophet Moses
Painted by the Author Ronald Rayner

Chapter 2

COMPARING THE RESULTS OF CONTACTING ALIENS THROUGH OUIJA BOARDS, TO THE EFFORTS OF DEDICATED MEDIUMS

If we compare the experiences of Jeff Hillier and his friends in the early days of public interest in the Alien Phenomena, and the results achieved by modern day professional mediums dedicated to contacting Aliens, it raises many interesting questions:

PREVIOUSLY – A BRIEF EXTRACT FROM, 'First Alien Contact', by Ronald Rayner, on Amazon Kindle.

A group of experienced practicing mediums gathered together at a spacious bungalow owned by their group lead medium, Mary White.

The group found themselves in contact with an Alien Star Ship, cloaked in our solar system. An Alien named Charm, was directing small saucer shaped craft from around the base of the Star ship, to abduct earthlings to harvest human DNA and Eggs, and return the abducted earthlings unharmed close to the area from which they were abducted.

The Star ship avoids any contact with Earth's governments. However, if their Star Ship were ever attacked, the Aliens have the capability of fetching everything on planet Earth to a standstill, thus paralysing the planet. However, Aliens apparently operate under strict code; not to harm any human type life, anywhere in our solar system. Unfortunately, word has leaked out to world Intelligence services that a group of British mediums are in contact with an Alien, which places the group in danger from the actions of sinister overseas intelligence services.

OUIJA BOARD AND ALIEN CONTACTS BY JEFF HILLIER

At the age of five, three small boys, Jeff (myself), Dave, and Kevin were destined to become lifelong friends. In 1954, we started school at the Infants of Montague Road, Edmonton. We were there for two years, having all the usual lessons for five- to seven-year-olds. In those days, we were given a third of a pint of milk each day and took a midday nap. Once, I pretended to not wake up, only to have the playground bell rung loudly in my ear. I also remember playing kiss chase during playtime, and making a pretty little blonde girl cry, I was too enthusiastic and banged her head against the wall, which upset me almost as much as it did her!

Our head mistress was Miss Guyford, a little bit formidable for five-year-olds. Our first year teacher was Miss Cox she was very nice, just right for young children. Our second and final teacher was Miss Luwellen, she was also very nice, very young, and very beautiful, she looked like the singer Kathrin Jenkins. On our last day at that school a lot of the children, especially the boys, lined up to kiss her goodbye. I was too shy and missed out!

It was 1956 when we progressed to the primary school at Bretenham Road, a late Victorian building with lots of character. My grandmother, Hilda, my mother, Reene, and Aunt Win all went there. Bruce Forsyth also attended the school a year or two after my aunt. The school photo which appeared in his autobiography was taken in exactly the same place as those of Reene and Win.
Although the school had electric lighting, our classrooms still had working gas lamps. They would be turned on during dull winter afternoons using a hooked pole needed to pull down a lever to light the four gas mantels in each lamp. One time, one of these mantels dropped, and disintegrated into a damp, white substance on a desk lid.

The next four years went by with all the usual incidents that occur with seven to eleven-year-olds. In those days there was the real threat of getting the cane. I managed to get away with only one caning, which really hurt! Others in our class were getting it far too often. Dave got a rap over the knuckles for no good reason, Kevin completed the four years unscathed, he was the quiet one.

Other much lesser punishments were to wipe the chalk off the black board, or to fill the ink wells in the desks with thick black ink that often needed to be watered down - most of us actually enjoyed the last two jobs. One time the ink was spilt and ran inside the desk unnoticed for days, it dried on some paper, the joker of the class carefully cut round the ink and placed it in the middle of the open class register, our class teacher, Miss Green was horrified at first, but soon saw the joke.

She was a great teacher. She took us in small groups on Saturdays to various educational places. I met up with my group at the Angel Edmonton, outside Pollocks, the camping shop diagonally opposite the Regal cinema. We went to the Tower of London, I remember seeing the Ravens, the Torture chamber, and the Crown Jewels. On another Saturday, Dave and Kevin's group went to the Natural History Museum.

As I remember, we didn't so much fail the Eleven Plus as we didn't get the chance to take it. I was a 'late developer', that's my excuse. Although, Dave has recently told me that he thinks we did sit the exam in the assembly hall. Anyway, without passing that exam, we had to return to the secondary modern part of Montague Road school.

This is when our interest in various subjects developed, we were, all three of us good at art and drawing. Kevin was particularly good at sketching the current Prime Ministers face. I remember him, with amusement, moaning when Harold Macmillan resigned, but it wasn't long before he had mastered Alec Douglas-Home, and later Harold Wilson's likeness. He was also very good at sketching futuristic cars and aircraft. Dave and I were interested in all forms of wildlife, from insects -especially lepidoptera - to birds, animals, and fish. We both kept Tropical Aquarium Fish for many years. I also liked to plant small native trees, shrubs, and wildflowers.

OUIJA BOARD CONTACTS

The one thing that all three of us were very interested in was Unidentified Flying Objects (UFOs), and Aliens. After four years, most of our classmates left, including Kevin, but Dave and I stayed on for a fifth year, and left school in 1965. For the last eleven years, we had, of course, met up on school days but this had now ended. To keep in touch, I would cycle to Dave's house less than five minutes away to meet up in the evenings once or twice a week.

In the mid 1960s, Ouija boards were sold as an entertaining and mysterious clairvoyant experience. Dave and I had one each. These boards were about 300mm x 450mm and printed with all the letters of the alphabet, the words 'Yes' and 'No', 'Goodbye', and the numbers 0 to 9. The board also included a message indicator or pointer (planchette) with a circular window to see the letters and numbers through. This pointer had three felt feet to aid sliding over the board and spelling out messages from the spirit world (there was a call from some religious authorities for these boards to be banned).
It was around 1967 when one evening, we decided to give the Ouija board a try. We sat on chairs facing each other with the board on our knees and one hand each resting lightly on the pointer. Following the suggested directions, I asked 'If anyone's there please go to yes'. On the second or third request the pointer would usually slowly go to yes. Over the years, I must have asked this question hundreds of times. On some occasions, when it was particularly slow, I would get tired of asking the questions and Dave would take over, it was very seldom that nothing happened. The next question would usually be 'who is there?', or 'please spell out your name? Most of the time the pointer would move surprisingly quickly, and glide smoothly over the board.
On this first occasion, the pointer circled over the letters and spelt out William Payne, who informed us that as he was our first contact he would be our guardian, and guide should we need him. In one session, William referred to God or a similar figure in the spirit world as 'Big Tom', a kind of controlling entity. We discussed this amazing contact; did we really believe we were conversing with the spirit of William Payne? I asked Dave if he was moving the pointer, he convinced me he wasn't, and I told him that I hadn't knowingly pushed it. We

decided to experiment, I asked Dave to think of a short sentence and spell it out, the result was totally different, my fingers kept losing contact with the pointer. I then tried to spell out a few words and the result was the same, and if either one of us took our fingers off the pointer, it would quickly grind to a halt.

As we were both in agreement that we were not consciously moving the pointer, the only other options were that we were both subconsciously moving it, or that it was, in fact, the spirit of William Payne, somehow telepathically making us move it. Regardless of whether this was a spirit led contact or not, there is no doubt that there was something extraordinary happening, whether it be telepathy, supernatural, or otherwise. There is also a third option, it is commonly believed by religious people, that other spirits, probably evil, are impersonating the named contacts (possibly the reason why they wanted the Ouija boards banned).

Over the years we had many contacts, sometimes it took several minutes or more before the pointer moved and would be quite slow, and other times it would be sliding vigorously across the board in perfect arcs and circles over each letter to be indicated. We had to be careful not to let our fingers slip off the pointer when it moved around that fast, otherwise it could fall off the edge of the board and interrupt the flow. We could quickly regain momentum when it was going at speed, but once our hands left the pointer it would cease to move. If it had moved, that would have probably been telekinesis.

There was one particularly memorable occasion when it spelt out 'please help me!' several times. We could sense the extreme agitation with this contact in the way the pointer moved around the board, vigorously and without pause. Despite asking for a name, the pointer continued to spell 'please help me'! but eventually after reassuring this contact we would get help, the name Pauline Saunders was spelt out. She told us she was in a very dark place, alone, and frightened, and she was very reluctant to lose contact with us. We told her that we would ask William Payne to help her, and that we needed her to relinquish contact before we could do that, as she kept persistently returning.

As soon as she left, we contacted William Payne and explained the situation, he said he would help but it wasn't until a few sessions later that he did. In the meantime, we again got 'please help me'! We went back and forth between William and Pauline. It took a couple more tries before she stopped pleading for help, we then assumed he had actually helped her, which he later confirmed he had. Fortunately, we never heard from her again. (Although, it would have been nice to know that she was happy).

Of all the many contacts we had, before and after, that one stands out as being the most convincing and incredible. It was a relief when she was finally helped. On making enquiries, Dave's Nan thought she may have been the victim of a direct hit from a bomb during the Second World War.

On another occasion, Dave's Aunt, Barbara sat in one of our sessions. After the usual 'who's there?' and 'please spell out your name', Barbara's father's name was spelt out. It was moving very strongly and so fast that Dave and I couldn't keep up with the wording or meaning of the message, (It was just a long string of letters to us) but Barbara was writing it down in a notepad, forming the words as she went. We could hear her gasping as the message appeared to her. It was as if her father had been given the opportunity to write a post card from the other side. He mentioned all the family that was there with him, even including the dog, and gave comforting messages for other members of the family not to worry about various problems, and incidents.

The message finished, and Barbara read it out to us. I certainly didn't know many of the family members mentioned, and Dave didn't know all of them. I believe Barbara was convinced the message was from her father, and not from us.

All these contacts occurred over 50 years ago in the mid to late 1960's. I wish I had asked to borrow that message and photocopy it. Sadly, over the years it was lost, but all the above is all as I recall it happening, without any exaggerations.

ALIEN CONTACTS

One evening we decided to visit Kevin as we hadn't seen him for a while, and he conveniently lived opposite Dave's house, so we took the Ouija board with us. We thought a session might keep us entertained for a few hours. We told him about all the contacts we had on the Ouija board and he was interested. He mentioned that his mother Violet and Aunt Kitty had one, and frequently used it for séances

On that evening, we made alien contact. Dave and I were seated as usual, with the Ouija board on our laps, and Kevin was sitting nearby observing. Up until that point, our previous contacts had been sluggish so we had lapsed into conversation. Our fingers were resting lightly on the pointer, so it was a surprise when, without the usual 'is anyone there?', the pointer began to move in circles around the middle of the board. This was the first time a contact had been made without asking. The thought crossed my mind that this could be an alien, and that the connection we had made was a telepathic one. He spelt out his name as Carantus.
--
'Where are you?'
'In my body'
'Where are you from?'
'The Planet Gramedia in the Galaxy Andromeda'
'Where are you now?'
'Flying Over'
'In a spaceship?'
'Yes'
'If we go outside, would we see you?'
'Yes'
'We're going to have a look. Will we be able to make contact again?'
'Yes'

We went out in the garden, it was dark, and after about twenty seconds, something which looked like a satellite in size and speed, passed over, and was in view for about a minute. We rushed back inside and regained contact with Carantus, he confirmed that the sighting was him. We continued conversing with him for about ten minutes until he had to go. He said we could contact him again by asking for him by name.

A few days later, we made our next contact with Carantus, and from then on, we always went to Kevin's to make contact. It wasn't long before Kevin's mum and dad became interested. Kevin's dad, Sid, would look in the newspaper to check the times when satellites were going over, to avoid any confusion with the space craft should it fly over, (which it did a few more times). Sid would also make a pot of tea for us, and anyone else that was there at the time, he made us feel very welcome.

The next time we went to Kevin's, he told us that he had contacted Carantus with his mother Violet, they had a very interesting session, and had conversed with a friend of Carantus named Saunus.

On another occasion, we happened to mention an interesting article in a scientific book that Kevin had been reading. Carantus asked to look at a few chapters in the book. He explained that all we had to do was to maintain contact, so Dave and I kept our fingers on the pointer, while Kevin sat nearby looking at each page. Carantus would then indicate to turn the page by moving the pointer to 'Yes'. Kevin only had to scan each page for a few seconds, and the pointer would quickly move to yes, those chapters and in fact, the whole book was soon finished.

Carantus, I think was trying to educate us, and was explaining the newly discovered facts about D.N.A. and other related subjects. Dave mentioned this to his dad Eric, who happened to be interested in D.N.A. and was reading up on the subject.

The next time we went to Kevin's, Eric came with us, and he wasn't disappointed. He had a long communication with Carantus, and was very impressed. Up until then he hadn't taken much notice when we told him of our contacts on the Ouija board, but now he took it much more seriously, as he knew that our knowledge on that subject was very limited.

On another occasion, there was quite a crowd of us, including Violet and Sid, and Kevin's older brother David and his girlfriend. During this contact with Carantus, he was asked what he looked like, he spelt out, that if we all held hands, he could send a kind of telepathic vision of himself.

Of course, we complied with his suggestion, and within a few seconds, Violet and Kevin received a strong vision of his appearance, the others also visualised a good likeness to the description given by Kevin and his mother.

His appearance was tall and athletic and wearing what looked like a one-piece suit and had medium to long fair hair. Dave said he had a vague impression of him, and I didn't really get much, but it did fit in with how I had imagined him to look.

On another occasion, the three of us decided to ask Carantus if we could join him in his space craft and to our surprise he said yes. There were no suitable locations anywhere near Edmonton, so our suggestion was Sailsbury Plain, as it mentioned in our U.F.O. books, there were a high number of sightings in that area. He said he would let us know when he could make arrangements for an exact location, and time to meet up.

This revelation prompted quite a discussion between us, would he make these arrangements, and turn up? Would we actually enter his space craft if he invited us to? We eventually agreed that we would. If he meant us any harm, he could easily do whatever he wanted anyway. The other question was would we 'chicken out' at the last minute? We were never to find out, as a 'meet up' was never mentioned again.

On another occasion, Dave was on a caravan holiday in Suffolk. One night, Dave and his aunt decided to contact Carantus. It was a good session as usual, and finished with 'I will be flying over now'. They went outside, it was a warm, clear night, and looking up they saw the light of the space craft. It was the usual appearance, except when it got overhead it stopped, and went back in the same direction it had just travelled! Dave, and especially his aunt was very impressed, as Satellites can't do that!

Dave, Kevin and I were discussing this appearance in Suffolk. I said that I hadn't seen anything more convincing than just a satellite type appearance, Kevin said he had recently seen the craft fly swiftly by, as a disk about the size of the full moon, which was much more impressive than any of my sightings.

Around about the spring of 1969, all three of us acquired our first cars, all Mini's. Daves was white, Kevins red, and my one was grey. These changed our lives, particularly for Dave and myself.

We started to go to Disco's and dance halls, such as the Tottenham Royal, or the Bird's Nest, at Muswell hill. As our interest in going out increased, our sessions on the Ouija board decreased to maybe once a week or less. Kevin's interest didn't wane, he kept the contacts going, it was around this time that he told us about a third alien, Polgairus.

Kevin and Violet had inadvertently made contact with him, and the session was strange, and unexpectedly cut short by Carantus. Polgairus was apparently a troublemaker. Carantus and Saunus advised Kevin to avoid any further contact with him if possible.

In July of that year, I went to Ibiza on a two-week family holiday with my parents, younger brother Stephen who was seventeen, Aunt Win, Uncle Tony, and my sixteen-year-old cousin, Colin - I was twenty.

On the first day after breakfast, it was, as expected, hot and sunny so we headed to the swimming pool. There were quite a few elderly Yorkshire women lounging on sun beds next to the pool, enjoying the weather in their floral summer dresses. Colin had, an unfortunate (for me) sense of humour. He ran along the edge of the pool and when he got alongside these women, he leapt as high as he could, tucked one knee under his arms and 'water bombed' them! I Was shocked that he could be that blatant, but imagine my embarrassment when he resurfaced and laughingly shouted, 'did I get them Jeff'!? (they were soaked) With implication that I was encouraging him! He then got out of the water and repeated the 'water bombing'. I left the pool area before he resurfaced.

Colin's parents inadvertently saved these women any further interference when they called him away to go to the local beach. We were staying at a hotel in the town centre, the nearest beach being a short ferry boat crossing. The hotel, therefore, gave free tickets to use the ferry so we all went to check this beach out. It was nice and sandy, at least a mile long, with sand dunes at the back, and there were Pedalo boats for hire.

Later, that afternoon, we went back to the hotel pool. The Yorkshire women, fortunately, had gone. Stephen and Colin were playing water volley ball with an inflatable beach ball. I decided to join in, and soon two girls began to throw the ball back when it went in their direction. They also joined in the game.

They were sisters, both attractive, Deborah looked about eighteen, and Tracey about thirteen. They were on the same two weeks holiday as us, also with their parents and grandparent. They were from Sheffield, Yorkshire. I was getting on very well with Deborah, she was easy to talk to, and we had a lot of similar interests. Time flew, and it was soon evening mealtime, (we were all on 'half board' with the hotel), we arranged to meet up by the pool later that evening.

It wasn't long before Deborah and Tracy joined us at the pool side. I got them a drink and they told us about their day. The conversation was easy, and time flew by. A little later, their parents joined us, we were all introduced, and they stayed for a few drinks, until it was time to leave for the night. Deborah said, "see you at breakfast time."

From the second day on, we were together all the time, except of course at night. Although one time, there was a 'late night Disco' we wanted to go to. I asked Joe, Debbie's, father, about going, he said yes, but no alcohol, and I would be responsible for her, we had a great time.

Every day was hot and sunny. We spent quite some time sunbathing and applying the lemon scented olive oil, which was on sale everywhere. We were 'frying ourselves' to get tanned, then swimming to cool off. I remember Debbie saying that it will save her dad paying for tights for her, for quite some time.

The days passed too quickly. A week had flown by. In the evening, towards dusk, we were looking round the shops near our hotel and there were a lot of people outside a Bar watching television.

We decided to see what was going on. As we joined them, we could sense the excitement. Everyone started cheering. The American's Apollo 11 had just landed on the Moon! That was a great event to end the day on, we stayed for a soft drink to join in with the celebrations, and then went back to the hotel.

The next day it was announced that Neil Armstrong was the first man to step foot on the Moon, saying those iconic words, 'One small step for man, one giant leap for mankind'. While the subject of Space travel was on the news, I thought it a good opportunity to mention Carantus, (not that I had given him much thought on the holiday). To my surprise Deborah was interested, and asked me all about the contacts that I had had with Dave and Kevin on the Ouija board, and could we try it? I was a little sceptical and said maybe.

After another lovely day on a white sandy beach close to the sea, Debbie mentioned contacting Carantus. I agreed that we could try to contact him after the evening meal, which would be a good time. Of course, we had no Ouija board, so the usual thing was to use a wall mirror, or similar smooth surface, an upturned glass as the pointer, and Debbie used her lipstick to write the letters and numbers down.

It started slowly at first, but soon spelt out 'yes' when I asked for Carantus. The glass was moving over the mirror nicely, we were asking all the usual questions, with good answers. He then spelt out he was with Suanus, and they had been monitoring the Moon landing, and that they had left an informative item of interest on the Moon for the Americans to find. Debbie then started talking in Latin (one of her school subjects) she was getting good replies back, also in Latin, this carried on for a few minutes, and eventually, Carantus said they had to go, and spelt out goodbye, in Latin, she was very impressed.

I had been a bit concerned that this contact might 'freak her out', as it sometimes did with 'first timers', but I needn't have worried, she was fine with it, and as I didn't speak Latin, she was convinced that I hadn't been pushing the glass. I think she was really pleased to have spoken to an Alien. I told her about my views on the subconscious etcetera, just in case she mentioned it to her parents. They never said anything to me, so I think she kept it to herself (there are many people, mostly religious that would disapprove, and not touch an Ouija board). The rest of the holiday went very well, even Colin eased off with his larking about. The last day soon came, and most of the hotel guests got on the coach for the Airport.

We soon got to the Airport, as usual there was a delay, I didn't mind, it extended the holiday a few hours. I took some more photos before we got on the plane. Luckily, I was able to sit next to Debbie, it was a short flight with no food provided, I asked the air hostess for some savoury biscuits (the only available food) which we shared with Tracey.

The plane arrived back at Luton, we collected our luggage, and went through customs. I remember seeing Deborah on the coach just before they set off back for Sheffield. She looked quite sad, we waved goodbye, and I never saw her again.

That last contact with Carantus in Ibiza was the end of all the significant contacts I had on the Ouija board. After that holiday, as I have said, Dave and I were going out more, but Kevin didn't want to join us. He continued to contact Carantus on the Ouija board with Violet and Kitty into the early 1980's. During that time they had a number of convincing sightings of the space craft, and some memorable conversations. Sometime after that he wrote down his memories of the contacts he had. To this day (early 2023) he believes in all those contacts, and that Carantus, Suanus, and probably Polgairus, are still around, Kevin had an extra ten years of convincing contacts. (As for Dave and me, we don't know, I would say we are 50-50 on it.)

OUR EXPERIENCES OF SPIRITUAL HEALING

After several months of going out to discos and dance halls, Dave met his future wife, Rita. I didn't so much lose a friend as gain one, as Rita also became a good friend, and (to this day) we all have a good laugh, on the phone and whenever we meet up.

Dave had now settled down (1970) I lasted out until May 1975, when Margaret moved into my recently purchased flat at Stamford Hill, I was now also settled. However, like the weather there were many unsettled intervals, I had a remarkable knack of unintentionally being annoying. This would cause a short spell of shouting from Margaret directed at me, and unfortunately one of the many cats we had acquired, 'Tim-Two' used to get even more upset than me! If he couldn't get out in time he would have an asthma attack. His nick name became 'Timid Tim'.

On one occasion, I must have been particularly annoying, prompting a tornado of verbal out bursts, poor Tim didn't get out in time, he had a very severe asma attack. He nearly died, he peed on the floor, was almost unconscious, and could barely breath. I couldn't help him breath in, but I could help him breath out by squeezing the air out of his lungs on each exhalation, until he slowly recovered. He was to be completely cured of these attacks years later by Spiritual Healing.

Back to 1972, Dave and Rita got married, I was Dave's 'Best Man', the Wedding celebrations went very well, and after their Honeymoon they returned to the house Dave grew up in, opposite Kevin's. By 1980 they had two children, Victoria and Spencer, and had moved out to Hoddesdon, Hertfordshire.

They soon settled in there, and after a few years (1983/84) Dave had joined a Spiritual Healing group, meeting up at 'Toc H', (an International Christian Movement) on Monday evenings, and attending a Spiritualist Circle on Wednesday evenings at Ashwell house Thunderidge.

Over the few years that Dave had been healing, he had probably seen dozens of patients with varying results. Sometimes there was a positive result, and other times it would have little effect, but there was never any harm done. The healing would simply be performed with the patient sitting on a chair, the healer would stand behind, and without any physical contact would hover their hands around the head and shoulder area of the patient. Some would attend for several weeks, most showing some improvement, a few might only go once. but on two occasions Dave had achieved some quite dramatically successful results.

On the first occasion, a woman came in, and after the initial greetings, she explained that she had severe back pain, and that it had been caused in a car crash several years before. As was usual, she sat in the chair while Dave carried out the healing, after four or five minutes, he said that should be enough. The woman bent over to pick up her handbag from the floor beside her and burst into tears.

For a split second, Dave thought 'what have I done'? The woman soon explained that she hadn't been able to bend like that without any pain since the accident, and that the tears were of emotional joy. She of course was very grateful and thanked Dave profusely as the pain had almost gone, she said she would return for another session.

The next week she did turn up, she was almost unrecognisable, she looked ten years younger, all the stress caused by the continual pain had gone. She had another session that evening, and was pain free, she didn't need to have any more healing.

On the other occasion a young woman came in with a rash on her face and neck, diagnosed as Psoriasis, she said it was covering her whole body, and that she had tried everything to get rid of it. Dave carried out the healing as usual, advised her to come back next week for more healing. She returned the following week looking very much happier, her face was clear of the rash, and she said it had also gone from most of her body, apart from the knees down. She had another healing session and didn't have to return again.

It was autumn of 1986 when my father had a prostate operation, he never recovered completely, but was well enough to start work again for a brief period. By the spring of 1987 he was complaining of a terrible taste in his mouth, and later a build up of fluid in his ears was making life extremely uncomfortable for him. His Doctor was doing nothing to relieve his symptoms, perhaps he didn't complain enough, I asked Dave if he would try some healing, he came that same day.

As feared it didn't do a lot of good, Dave suggested it might be cancer, which hadn't occurred to me, but was an obvious diagnosis. Dave had done all he could, and before he left he gave me a copy of Psychic News, which contained a list of spiritual healers. Harry Corran's name stood out, he lived in Chigwell, and after contacting him, it was arranged for him to come the next day. In the meantime I wrote a letter to the doctor explaining how the symptoms my father had were getting worse, and he needed to be sent to hospital without delay for investigations.

Harry arrived at mum and dad's place, a two bed maisonette at the back of the Regal cinema Edmonton. He had a sympathetic conversation with dad, then carried out the healing, there was little or no improvement, it turned out that dad had a particularly aggressive form of cancer. There was not much more Harry could do for him.

I then mentioned that Margaret had a recurring ear infection that her Doctor had advised would require an operation in the near future. On Harry's suggestion, it was arranged for him to visit us the next day, at Highams Park, to try the healing on Margaret, as usual, it only took a few minutes, we were then chatting 'over a cup of tea', and Timid Tim happened to be sitting beside us. I mentioned the asthma attacks that he still suffered from, so Harry picked him up and sat him on his lap for a few minutes, and gently stroked him, that was it, Tim never had another attack, and lived happily for many years after. (Even though I couldn't stop being annoying).

In the meantime, the letter to the Doctor had resulted in dad being admitted to St. Barts. Hospital, where he got immediate relief from his symptoms. The prognosis however was not good, it was confirmed that the cancer was very aggressive, and he only had about three weeks. Dad passed, it was mid-July, he was only sixty-four and didn't even get his pension.

It was nearly a decade later that Margaret eventually had to have the ear operation. It went well and she soon made a good recovery, better than the original predictions. All things being considered I believe there's a lot to be said for the effectiveness of Spiritual Healing. (it's always worth a try).

DOPPELGANGER

Back to Autumn 1948, my parents were looking for a place to live. I was on the way, (due date late April) so in the meantime, my grandad, Jim asked his first World War friend, Arthur Frisby, if he could help. 'Art', lived a four or five minute walk from grandad's, in Lawrence Road Edmonton. They were old terrace houses backing on to Craig Park. He was living next door to his sister Amy, and 'brother in-law' known as Blackman who owned both houses. It was agreed that Arther would keep the two front rooms, and my mum and dad would have the rest of the house; two bedrooms, a living room, kitchen/scullery, and outside toilet (no bathroom). My dad only paid one pound a week rent for nearly two decades, right up until we left due to planned demolition. Most of the houses on that side of the street were cleared to become an addition to Craig Park.

I was born 25 April 1949, and unbeknownst to me at the time, my first lifelong friend, Will lived next door, with his parents and older sister, Annette. He was seven months older than me.

Arthur was like a grandad to me. I soon got to know his routine. He would have to carry his bucket of 'slops' (as he called it) to the toilet. He would knock on the door, and state the obvious "it's only me", then go through our living room and kitchen, (sometimes slopping the contents) to the outside toilet. (that's how many families had to live in those days).

It was about 1964, Arthur would have been around seventy-four when he was admitted into North Middlesex Hospital for about ten days because of a chest ailment. One evening before he was discharged, we heard the familiar rattling of his keys in the front door lock, (shaky hands) then his heavy steps (he wore hobnail boots) along the passageway to our living room door, he didn't knock to say "it's only me" as he usually did, but instead went straight up the stairs to his bedroom. We could hear him moving around, nothing unusual, and after about three or four minutes he closed his door and came down the stairs we could hear every step so clearly. He got to the bottom, but didn't knock to say anything as we were expecting him to, but walked back down the passageway opened the front door and closed it behind him, pulling on the old cast-iron doorknob to make sure it was shut, as usual, (apart from a small recess, the front door opened straight onto the footway).

Before he had finish shutting the door, Mum said "that's funny, he should still be in hospital, and he didn't even say anything". I quickly got up and ran to the front door to have a look. He had vanished. If he had gone next door to Amy's, we would have heard him, and he wouldn't even have had time to get there (he was getting very slow and doddery on his feet). If he had gone back in the direction of the hospital, he would have only just got past Will and Annette's house by that time, so it was a mystery.

When he came home from hospital, Mum asked him why he had come back that evening, and how had he got out of the hospital and back in again without the nurses knowing. He denied that he had left, saying he was barely well enough to get out of bed. Mum later said that she thought he lied because he didn't want to get into trouble for leaving without permission or being discharged, but he knew we wouldn't have said anything, and he was by then discharged anyway. (no need to lie)

It's a long walk to the hospital, and not much shorter by bus, I don't think he could have walked it, and don't think he would ever use a taxi, that would have been extremely unlikely and doesn't explain his vanishing act. He could never have climbed into a taxi in that time. There are only two other possible explanations, one would be an actor who had studied Arthur's movements to the smallest detail and took his place that evening for some obscure reason. Or it was Arthur's Doppelganger looking for something in his bedroom.

For me, the whole event remains a mystery, but if Doppelganger's are a possible phenomenon, then I would have to say that is the most likely explanation. I believe that they are supposed to materialise, leaving the original body unaware and in some kind of reduced state, and can then vanish back, re-entering the body again. If that is a possibility, then it would explain all that we witnessed that evening.

TELEKINESIS

Forward again to 1986, around the time my dad became unwell. We had spent ten (unhappy for Margaret) years at Stamford Hill, and moved in the Spring of 1985, to Gordon Avenue, Highams Park, with our four-month-old daughter, Jennifer, and six cats. All had been strays. Margaret would never have left them. These cats proved to be a Nemesis for our new elderly next door neighbour, John Frazer, (he had a Fushia named after him) He was an avid prize-winning horticulturist, and World War veteran. The cats, among other things, had dug up all his prized carrots! (Despite us providing them with cat litter).

The new house was much bigger than the flat we had just left, so we often went to 'Epping Antiques' (now Lathams) looking for furniture. We got quite friendly with the owner, Peter Hellmers. He had six children and would jokingly say "I tried it six times and decided I didn't like it". We had already purchased several items from him by the time we saw the large satinwood wardrobe that we both really liked. It still had the price tag on it. I soon found Peter and said we would have it. He immediately apologized, saying "sorry I should have taken the price tag off, it was sold this morning".

We were really disappointed. He said "give me your phone number. I don't think they were sure that they wanted it". Within a few days Peter phoned up and told me they had change their mind about the Wardrobe, and we could have it. A week later it was up in our front bedroom, and full of clothes.

One night in early summer of 1986, when Jennifer was about eighteen months old, I was woken by a loud bang. The room was almost pitch black, a little light filtered through the curtains from the streetlamp outside. I could just see that Jennifer was asleep in her cot next to me, Karla our Colly dog was in the corner of the room next to the wardrobe, not responding to the bang, and Margaret was still asleep.

Maybe the bang wasn't so loud as I had thought and was amplified in my head. As all seemed well, I went back to sleep. In the morning Margaret got up and said "what's this doing here on the floor?" She was about to pick up the bottom draw from the wardrobe. I remembered the loud bang, and said "no leave it", I wanted to have a good look at it, before it was replaced. It was full of clothes and had come out dead square. The back of the drawer was at least two feet out from the front of the wardrobe, it had therefor been ejected forward by about four feet, then dropped onto the floor, hence the loud bang. I can't explain how it happened, no one could have possibly got into the house to do that, and for what possible reason? I would have seen and heard them, and there was no forced entry. I still find it hard to believe that it happened, I have no logical explanation for it, and telekinesis isn't an appropriate explanation for it either.

That incident was nearly thirty-seven years ago, and nothing like it has happened since, except about six years later our second daughter Jessica, told Dave and Rita, (on one of their visits), that she has two little girls to play with in her bedroom. On prompting, Rita found out that they were 'play mates' for Jessica and that they were dressed in Victorian clothing. Jen and Jess, at that time shared the room with the Satinwood wardrobe in, (although Jennifer never mentioned seeing the girls), maybe the apparition of these girls had some connection to the incident with the drawer.

ALIENS AND THE INTERDIMENSIONAL REALITY OF THE PARANORMAL FIT TOGETHER LIKE HAND AND GLOVE

Our title is confirmed by comparing two true stories, the first from Author Jeff Hillier in his school days over half a century ago when he, and two school friends, made contact with an Alien using 'Ouija Boards.
The second true story recorded in recent times by author Ronald Rayner from his recent book 'First Alien Contact', tells the story of a group of close dedicated experienced mediums coming together a few days every week, who was in contact with an Alien Star Ship dedicated to abducting humans to harvest eggs and sperm in order to breed interplanetary Aliens that will be infiltrated into high government office on planet Earth, plus their experiences with the 'Men in Black'. The Star Ship avoids contact with Earth's governments, and made it clear that if their ship were ever attacked by Earth's governments "They have the capability of fetching everything on planet Earth to a standstill, thus paralyzing every activity on the planet". However, the Aliens in question assured us that they act under a strict code: not to harm any evolved human life, anywhere in the Solar System. Unfortunately, word leaked to World Intelligence Services that a group of British Mediums is in contact with an Alien Ship, which places the group in danger from

the actions of sinister overseas intelligence services.

CHAPTER 3

Standing outside Number 10 Downing Street, the residence of the British Prime Minister, a driver was looking at his watch, coincident with the Prime Minister exiting Number 10 and a Prime Minister advisor arriving breathless at the car. Unusually the Prime Minister sat beside the driver urging his adviser and personal protection officer to sit in the rear seats. The adviser leaned forward and spoke into the Prime Minister's ear "Sir, did you hear the news this morning on Radio Four?"

"Yes, I always listen to the news on Radio 4 whilst I am preparing for work, but to what are you referring specifically?"

" Well sir, I have seen you reading books by author Ronald Rayner, a world authority on the paranormal and leading visionary, who is said to be heading a group of mediums who are in contact with an alien."

"Get to the point man I am in a hurry"

"Well sir, the alien has admitted that an alien craft is abducting humans to harvest their human DNA and eggs, apparently the rarest and most sought after elements in our Solar System and essential to the survival of their own race, returning the abductees unharmed after enduring the trauma of a scary event. Separate from the survival of their alien race, aliens are accelerating the development of interplanetary humans to infiltrate governments on planet Earth. Then followed a warning from the alien, if fighter aircraft from various governments ever discovered their starships 'cloaked' in the Solar System, and attacked, they have the technology to fetch economies across planet Earth to a complete standstill; close airports, power stations, fetch trains and roads to a standstill and so on"

"Go on, go on" said the Prime Minister "fascinating, fascinating, and of national importance. Walk with me until we reach the House of Commons."

" When questioned by a reporter Sir, Rayner said, "no comment" and since he always speaks the truth I personally believe that means a loud 'yes', Prime Minister."

"Go on man more, more".

"The aliens claim that author Ronald Rayner is the only lay scientist on planet Earth who fully understands that Earth is comprised of two dimensions, the first; a Physical Dimension explained by Professor Einstein, mass, energy, speed of light, with a flawed instantaneous described as "the smallest distance between two points", the Other Dimension, the Paranormal, a mass less non physical, instantaneous reality where time just is, thus in the paranormal its possible to move backwards and forwards in time to produce a synchronicity. The paranormal has a paranormal shadow, recording for every human being, their everything that ever was, and ever will be dissolving on death producing the judgement before reincarnation with repentance included".

"Good God, go on, this is fascinating stuff, and possibly of national importance. Stay in the car with me to the House of Commons. Why is it that although I read Rayner's books I don't know anything about this?"
"Although Rayner is a successful lay scientist Sir with an impeccable record of predicting future events, banging on about global warming in his books for the last ten years, and the Covid Pandemic, he avoids publicity, and does not normally talk to the press, radio or tv, neither would most of the media understand what is writing about."
"Absolutely fascinating, talk to MI5 in my name."
"They are aware of him Sir, he was one of the key agents on the Independence of Ukraine, working with the CIA, KGB and Chinese Secret Police because Margaret Thatcher told MI5 and MI6 not to get involved. Rayner worked with the Ukrainian Ambassador in London and was our eyes and ears, recorded in his book, Joseph Escapes to Glastonbury.
" Find out everything you can and report back to me personally and see if you can get Rayner on the phone".
" I have him now, Sir."
" Ronald, how is it possible for the human mind to connect to an alien mind?"
"It can only be achieved Sir, through the channels of the paranormal instantaneous communication to anywhere in our Universe."
"I am not going to pretend to understand what you are saying Rayner, but what is the latest?"
"Right Sir, aliens have produced an interplanetary alien child from human DNA, and are improving its brain by increasing numbers of neurons and accelerating growth. The alien plan is to infiltrate their interplanetary humans into high office in government - for the only reason to keep watch over our inferior race of humans in order to ensure the survival of human kind".
"What do aliens think about us in the UK, Ronald and our American cousins?"
"Aliens regard us as clearly 'backward' because we use only a small part of the true potential of our brain, leaving us captured in crime, gluttony, sex additiction, drunkeness; greed and reluctant to do a full weeks work. The aliens on the other hand use chemical stimulation and mind training from the age of three years old when engrams are first laid down in order to use their brain in the most efficient working capacity, as it continues to grow. Aliens also regard Earth as having really inferior races of earthlings, whose beliefs leave them captured many years into their past. The next stage in alien development, Prime Minister, is absolutely fascinating. Having reached mind clarity and super intelligence, aliens realised they did not have to remain mortal and die, they could become immortal, live forever as alien cyborgs, part human and part indestructible self repairing robots. Put simply the process required a human type mind to be infused into the robot, which then becomes a Cyborg. It is amazing, Prime Minister, that in all this, aliens have never let go of their innate knowledge that there is a super power across the universe, knowledge that pervades every alien brain. Aliens also say that a human spirit continues through time and eternity, passing through any judgement

recorded in their paranormal shadow. Very important is their statement that the alien gods prohibit the killing of any humanoid, particular type one humans such as earthlings and themselves.""Aliens will never kill, they will prefer to suffer themselves in order to bring about change through persuasion and attention". "I am sorry gentlemen that I do not understand what that means." " What I do know is they are searching the Solar System for Type One Human DNA, apparently the rarest most sought after commodity in the entire universe". "Thank you Rayner, I must go now".

That evening, the group meeting was planned as usual. When everyone arrived and was seated, seance leader, Mary, explained that she had been drawn to speak to the alien because he wanted to get something important off his mind to be explained to everyone in the group when they arrived. Mary went on to explain why aliens are in search of human DNA because Type One life is very rare in the universe and in their race to become immortal, aliens were transferring their brain and mind into a robotic cyborg not realising that they would slowly lose their human DNA, and without replacing their DNA they would end up physically dead, and whilst its robot may last forever, they, the cyborg would cease with the loss of their reincarnation and eternal life. Thus their soul is lost and their existence through time and eternity is gone forever.

Mary addressed Redman Rayner, their organiser and titular head. "The information that aliens have revealed to us, Redman, is of crucial importance. Perhaps we should be contacting the government's television news channels and the national press". Redman jumped to his feet, "listen everyone, whilst I apologise for disagreeing with Mary, firstly the main danger is their press would look at us individually, and build us up so they could knock us down with the title of 'crackpots'. Secondly, publicity would attract the attention of other international sources that could put us in danger. We need to safeguard ourselves by making a trip to the Ministry of Defence. Nevertheless, we cannot deny that we have made one of the biggest breakthroughs in human history, the first ever communication with an alien on a starship in our Solar System. I believe that from now onwards the word secrecy is the key word, because it's not impossible that our group holds the key to the future of mankind on Earth. Raise your hand whoever is willing to make a trip to the Ministry of Defence building place. No one. Thank you."

"Before we break, I want to share my suspicion that we are being watched. There is always a grey Mercedes close by when we leave. Please don't be alarmed. I suggest that we should arrive for our meeting together and please, please note on
your phone anything that looks suspicious, including the grey Mercedes and the occupants. Until tomorrow everyone, and let us keep in touch with each other by phone".

"Mary, before you leave, could you spare 15 minutes to go over with me the theory that perhaps, our friends do not quite understand . Take a seat while I squeeze some more coffee from the pot. There you are, ready to drink, both of us without added sugar. Mary, what we know for certain is that of all the thousands of reported UFO sightings over the years there are probably only a couple of hundred sightings that even the military are unable to explain. This is where we, as a small independent lay group of enthusiasts have the advantage. As strange as that may sound, here is my reasoning. As a lay scientist, we, the group, are not bound by the conventions that influence the actions of military personnel. Our minds can venture into areas that would embarrass the military and its high ranking officers if they were seen 'to go there', such as clairvoyance for example, alien craft for another and thirdly the indestructible, self repairing cyborgs because, we as a group are uniquely aware that they are connected to the paranormal, and future time, and perhaps other close dimensions. This is why we have the advantage over the military and everyone else. I want you to think about this Mary, in your capacity as a teacher. I firmly believe that the clues to finding answers to some mysterious questions may lie in comparing the two future times, the physical dimension where Einstein rules, where everything is confined by the laws of physics, and the time is calculated and fixed. All compared to the shadow, non physical paranormal dimension, harmless, instantaneous over 360 degrees where time just is, historic present or future, where a synchronicity is instantaneous from anywhere in time or space. Think on these things Mary as a teacher, and let's put our heads together to hopefully come up with some plausible answers. Must go now Mary to my building site otherwise the men will be sitting around chatting.

"I am sorry to call you so early Redman, I guess you are with your men on your development site."
"Everything is fine Mary, I have just finished. What is so urgent?"
" Well we missed you last night, and no phone call."
"Sorry Mary, I developed the sniffles and when I arrived home went straight to bed. It paid off because I am fine now Mary."

"We made the most amazing breakthrough last night, Redman.I arrived late at the bungalow, and fortunately everyone had let themselves in and were eating fish and chips. They treated me to cod and chips, my favourite. The men shared your meal. Within forty five minutes there were five of us around the main table and I was calling upon alien. Communication was not perfect but from what I could make out alien wants us working tonight with a computer, and I can't wait to discover what this request is going to fetch. Redman please, please, come along early before the seven pm start.

Redman stood on his building site thinking about his plan to build super insulated, low maintenance, wheelchair friendly bungalows but found after speaking to

Mary he just could not concentrate. Redman gave up, stepped into his car and set off home to freshen up and change before setting off for Mary's bungalow, to arrive before the rest of the team. As Redman entered the front door Mary grabbed him with a vicelike grip, and gave him a kiss on the lips that seemed to go on forever. Sorry Redman I am so excited and really missed you last night.

Mary greeted everyone at the door of her large bungalow and directed them to the main room. A very large room with an impressive long highly-polished oak table, with a smaller table acrossways at the far end, behind which was a mini grand piano, above which hung a portrait of Moses. Redman, standing upright with shoulders back in true military style, was entertaining everyone with more clean jokes than anyone on the planet. Mary spoke up. "Thank you Redman, save a couple for me.You know the rules everyone, no smoking at any time, or puffing on an empty pipe John, and we do not raise the wine glasses until after the seance." Redman stood and said a short prayer, asking God for protection from evil spirits during their seance. Redman sat down and Mary opened. "Please everyone, concentrate on thinking about the alien, push aside any odd stray thoughts that wander into your mind." There was a quiet hush in the room. Mary spoke, "hands palm down on the table." Everyone placed their left hand gently on top of the person's hand seated on their left. "Eyes closed everyone." Mary spoke pointedly "alien alien, alien, alien friend, please communicate with us in this room at this time." There was silence and Mary spoke again, "alien, alien please communicate with us earthlings sitting round this table." A short pause, then Mary began speaking in a strange voice, a computer-like haunting manner. Obviously the alien was communicating through Mary. "Yes, I hear you alien. We are touching hands with those on either side. Now I must move my right hand onto my laptop computer in front of me on the table, and my left hand on the computer mouse, and I will continue tapping any key on the computer continuously until the alien says stop." Mary stopped and everyone sat up. "Listen everyone, the alien says I must take my bank laptop with me tomorrow as usual and upload everything into the bank's computer, after which whatever is on my computer will be wiped. I will do what the alien asks of me tomorrow and we will all meet here at 7pm. Now drink up the wine and dip into my lean beef sandwiches with english mustard."

Redman arrived home near midnight but needed to stay awake to deal with invoices and company cheques that needed to be paid into his company bank account in order not to lose his impeccable reputation. When Redman dragged himself up the stairs to his bedroom it was around 1am. Redman woke at 8am. No stranger to speaking to himself he was uttering, "Come on man, get ready and get out to your offices in the City of London."

When Mary arrived at work she uploaded her computer into the main banking system without a thought in her head that alien may be planning to control the world banking system. Suddenly the thought struck Redman, Mary is going to upload material into the world banking system. In a state of panic he rang Mary. No reply, no reply, what can I do? God, please help me. I'll drive to Mary's place of work in the City and try to get her to come out to lunch and persuade her not to do what she is planning. Redman drove to the city, which took two hours to travel 30 miles. He arrived at the Bank "Sorry, Mary is at another branch on a computer course" said the consulate at the bank door. What a waste of two hours, thought Redman. I must calm down. Of course Mary would not upload her computer as instructed by the alien Charm. Everything is ok. I will be meeting everyone at Mary's house at 7pm.

Redmans mobile rang. It was Mary "what's wrong Redman, I hear you tried to take me to lunch. Thank You, I'm sorry we missed each other, Must go", said Mary, "I have all the shopping to buy."
" Wait Mary, did you upload your computer into the banking system?"
" Yes, that's what my course was about. Everyone helped me to upload it. No one asked any questions, and it was a hundred percent successful. Sorry Redman must go shopping or there will be no coffee and sandwiches tonight."

Arriving home Redman sat and meditated for half an hour, because he firmly believes there is a form of consciousness in the unconscious, a psychic consciousness. Then he remembered that in his books, visionary Ronald Rayner has predicted what is happening now. Redman pinched his wrist to see if it was all a dream. Before deciding to shower, shave change and leave for Mary's bungalow and hopefully good cheer.

Over the chatting around the seance table Redman spoke up. " Listen everyone, I am becoming a little concerned about our own personal positions. We have quite innocently contacted an alien source through the paranormal who persuaded us to upload material into the UK Banking System that has access to every banking system across the world. I believe we need to tell someone in authority, quietly and discreetly, explain the bare bones of what has happened. That an alien entity has contacted us through our sessions and mediumship. That's the whole situation in a nutshell. What does the group think about my suggested approach? Good, I am glad everyone agrees with me. Now Mary, I want you, for your own safety, to be especially cautious. Tomorrow, leave the computer you have been using at work. Would it be possible for you to fetch home from your bank an almost identical laptop." "Yes I can do that, and I feel that under these strange circumstances we have quite inadvertently found ourselves in, we need to worry about our own position and safety." "All agreed, good. Now we need one of us, a volunteer, to go to the Ministry of Defence Building and explain that we have been in contact with an alien entity through the paranormal. What about you Roger? There are only three men in the group, and (we don't want the ladies involved,) plus that fact, no offence, (you are the oldest member of our group). Probably the best prepared to deal with this situation but, please do not mention uploading Mary's computer. Let us head home now and meet again tomorrow at 7pm. Then we will know Roger, whether 'they' have looked you up or allowed you to visit us tomorrow at 7pm. Good night everyone."

Next morning, whilst eating porridge topped with washed and sliced strawberries, Redman's phone rang at eight sharp. "That's Roger isn't it? How can I help? " I don't feel sufficiently confident to visit the Ministry of Defence. I'm sure I will make a mess and give away too much." " If you feel like that Roger I am glad you called me. I will go myself tomorrow around 10am. See you tonight."

The Next day, the taxi dropped Redman outside the entrance to the Ministry of Defence building, just after 10am. Uniforms were coming and going as Redman walked up to the reception desk. "What's the name Sir"
"Lord Redman Rayner."
"Good, how can I help your Sir?"
" I've had an encounter with an alien, and I would like to discuss the matter with someone perhaps in your alien department."
"Excuse me Sir, but let us not joke around, as you see I am busy, how can I help?"
" I have told you precisely the purpose of my visit, now can we get on please".
"Right, stand there, and I will call a commissioner to stand with you Sir, whilst I go and confer". He returned in a few moments "right Sir the commissionaire will accompany you to an office on the roof of the building where you can make your statement." Redman literally went outside over the roof along a railed walk-way and into a very large office covered wall to wall with cabinets containing hundreds of files. A very polite, well spoken man in a city suit, took Redmans details, name, address, and the address at which seances are held. He then wrote down the details of the alien contact all with a blank expression giving nothing away. The man looked up, thanked Redman for informing the Ministry of Defence about a supposed alien contact. A commissionaire accompanied Redman to the exit of the building. Redman was pleased with the simplicity of the whole preceding and jumped into a cab to his office.

That evening everyone was in good spirits, and clapped with three hoorahs after Redman told them about his visit to the Ministry of Defence." I hope you did not tell them about us" said John Poulter jokingly. "In future I think I will wear a moustache and beard, " said Mary.

"I love all of you, '' said Redman "but let us get down to business, over to you Mary."

Following the usual procedures Mary started speaking in her alien voice." Please tell me alien, from where are you speaking to us?"
"Sorry Mary, it would not be appropriate to reveal that information at this time, but I will tell you what I am allowed to say. I am part human and part android. My mind was transferred from my Type One human body into an indestructible self

repairing robot body. A small amount of fluid is all that is necessary to keep me functioning. It is possible for me to become human again by taking over another person's body in a form that you would describe as 'possession'. Then I could mate with a female and produce a transhuman alien. My race on my home planet are slightly smaller but more sturdy than earthlings, also pale skinned because our sun rays are weaker than on planet Earth. We have a Mother Ship 'cloaked' in the Solar System beyond the reach of Earth's missiles and aircraft, with small landers round the skirts of our ships. We aliens will not allow anything to get in the way of our harvesting human DNA and eggs from the females of the species, the scientific information from which is relayed back to our home planet and used on our Mother Ships, described by humans as our Star Ships. We send the small craft from our Star Ship to prepare chosen subjects in the USA, United Kingdom, and elsewhere. In the main, abductees experience, in the first instance, a paranormal abduction, as it would be explained on Earth, and from the experiment we choose those suitable for physical abduction to enable us to collect human DNA and eggs before returning the abductees relatively unharmed, except for minor mental trauma that is treatable by Earth's doctors. We do not see, or understand, the absolutely hostile reaction to what we are doing by Earth's military. When looked at in the light of abducting a few humanoids from a population of seven billion humans across the world we are comforted by the fact that no one believes the stories of the abductees, what helps is that Earth's military can't quite make up their minds about the truth of alien abductions and 'err' towards non belief. We are now looking at the UK and Europe for abductees because they are equal to, or sometimes superior, to United States citizens. We aliens ignore the inferior races on planet Earth, some captured many years in their past history, and may never realise their full potential. The biggest danger to the survival of earthlings is nuclear war and the global warming cycle, now triggered, will run its full course, as on other earth-like planets such as our own. More rain, more flooding, sea levels rising. An extinction level event.

We are smaller with pale skins, but with bigger lungs than earthlings. This is because our gravity is more intense even though we are further from our ancient main star, our sun and our atmosphere has less oxygen than on planet Earth. At an early age, our children are injected with growth chemicals to increase height, and to increase brain size to enable the stimulation of more neurons, for improved intelligence. We are surprised at the inadequacies of Earth Governments. Global heating is absolutely predictable, so is flooding, the extent of flooding and where the flooding will take place. Earth's scientists can predict these events and yet many people die needlessly because Governments do not put in place what is necessary to prevent flooding, damage to infrastructure and many deaths.
Another case is not examining in detail what actions need to be taken to protect earthlings from pandemics. Please do not gain the impression that we aliens are indestructible. Our personal code of conduct prohibits the killing of any humanoid,

even in protecting ourselves, because humanoids have an absolutely indisputable right of life, by the Power of the Universe for, Time and Eternity, albeit the selfish and the wicked will spend time with the unredeemed dead as punishment for the life they chose. Punishment beyond their comprehension. Your priestly classes, who commit sin and believe they can excuse themselves from this punishment, will be punished more severely than others."

Alien broke off his long discourse and everyone gasped as a strange powerful green hue covered the room, and the impression that a figure, an alien-like entity of some kind had just left the room pervaded everywhere with echoing words "don't be afraid, we will protect you." Mary looked up, her eyes streaming with tears saying "it's real, it's bloody real and I feel a little afraid." Redman stood and walked over to Mary. "Now Mary you heard the aliens promise, they will protect us Mary. A force more powerful than anything on planet Earth."

Mary stood, composed herself and whispered in Redmans ear, "Don't ever leave me Redman, promise you won't ever leave me". She looked round at everyone and said, "That's enough for one night. I'll pour a small nightcap for everyone before you leave". Strangely, everyone remained silent as they put down their glasses and said goodnight to Mary, giving her a small loving hug. As they left Mary looked at Redman "Why don't you stay the night Redman?" Redman looked into Mary's eyes. "Thank you sincerely Mary, but I must go, I have so much to attend tomorrow. You will be ok, I promise you. Ring me anytime".

After finishing his porridge with fresh strawberries, plus egg on toast, with a rasher of bacon and a cup of coffee, Redman's edwardian clock struck eight am. Redman felt an overwhelming need to call Mary, to help relieve her personal anxiety about the latest information from the alien.

"Good morning Mary."
" Hello Redman, this is a pleasant surprise."
" Mary, we both need to come together in thinking how we can persuade our friends to consider ways of protecting ourselves personally. The rather scary information given to us by the alien Mary, leaves us vulnerable to being accused of being a shadowy organisation conspiring with a foreign entity to harm British interests."
" Great idea Redman. We both need to put on our thinking caps to come up with a plan. Bye darling. See you tonight, but you can call me at work ". By the time Mary had voiced the idea of having lunch together, Redman had rung off.

That night Redman was the first to stand and address everyone round the seance table.
"I want everyone to look at Mary sitting all composed in her seat at the head of the table. Please tell us Mary, in detail, the events that took place whilst on your

way to work this morning."

" Well everyone, just like a James Bond movie, I was walking from the tube station to my office when a large 4x4 with darkened windows pulled into the curb, just in front of me. Two men jumped out calling "Hello Mary, Redman would like a word with you". They each grabbed one of my arms pulling me hastily into the rear seats of the vehicle. I was too surprised to think about calling out for help. One man placed his hand gently over my mouth whilst the other went through my bag and took out the laptop computer. The other man removed his hand from my mouth, pulled out a roll of money from his pocket, counted out £1500 in fifty pound notes, forcibly pushing it into my handbag. The other man said " right Mary, we are buying your computer for triple the value. This is no robbery, you are an intelligent woman, just keep quiet about this incident. Don't go to the police because they will not believe you. You are into something over your head. Remember we know where you work and live. Say anything to anyone, bad things will happen to you, possibly serious injury, if you know what I mean. Get out now, go to work and tell them you lost your computer on the tube train, off you go, and keep quiet". I stepped from their jeep. I was a bit shaken up and decided to buy a coffee to help a quick recovery. I was nearly half an hour late for work, but I made the excuse that the computer was missing from my bag and I went back to the station to ask if it had been handed in to lost property."

"Mary, we are all so sorry, how are you feeling now?"

"Thanks for asking everyone but I am ok. The fifteen hundred quid was a 'godsend, 'I received a letter in this morning's post from my bank asking me to call to discuss my unauthorised £1500 overdraft."

" Mary, which computer did they take?"

" Fortunately Redman, it was an old bank computer. The computer containing our data is hidden at work, and because of the mass of computers there, no one would ever be able to identify my computer."

"I thought it wise for me not to go to the police and tell them everything, and give them the money because these men are clearly secret government agents who have absolute authority over the police. However, I am paying the money into my bank account to clear my overdraft. I don't feel guilty, because I was abducted, my computer stolen or bought. The £1500 I was given is scant compensation for the trauma I have suffered. If these secret agents knew what we had learned recently from our alien, I can't think what else may have happened to me. I am feeling very tired now, everyone. Thank you for coming. Drink your glass of wine before you leave."

Next evening Mary laid out glasses of white wine and scones for everyone. With all seated, Mary raised her glass " please drink a toast with me. I want to show that I love you as my brothers and sisters.Thank you. Now I am asking Redman to summarise the position in which we find ourselves through no fault of our own, but please, if you have anything to add, please join in.,"

" My contacts tell me we have been rumbled as far up the chain as the Prime

Minister, Ministry of Defence, including the men in black. I also gain the impression that they believe we know more than the information we have shared with them, but I am, however, comforted that they may not believe anything we say. They may even suspect that we have invented the whole thing. The proof of my statement is Mary being abducted in broad daylight while walking to her office, and her computer taken, all taking place after we endeavoured to share our experience with a government department. We alone know that everything we have shared with the Ministry of Defence is true, but they are clearly sceptical about the veracity of our story, and our intentions, perhaps more particularly because we are close to internationally famous author Ronald Rayner, who was a key man in the Independence of Ukraine from Russia".

Mary stood. "Now everyone, this is important. I have raided our members' cash boxes to give each of you a gift of £100 pounds cash. From today you must use your mobile phone only for communication with work etc. Take the money I am about to give you and buy a 'pay as you go' phone. Give a false name and address if necessary when purchasing your new phone. Use it only when communicating with each other because your own personal mobile phone is certain to be tapped by the men in black. I suggest that we settle down and concentrate whilst I contact alien, to explain our dilemma, and confusion, about the problems we face, and ask them to protect us in any way they are able. Twenty minutes elapsed, eyes began to open accompanied by the fidgeting of legs and arms."

"No luck tonight. We can now relax and finish our wine and sandwiches."

Early next morning Mary's phone rang. "Hello Mary, I am going to be a little late tonight because I have to collect my car from the repairers."
" What's happened Redman?" asked Mary.
"An amazing story Mary, I want you to relay to the group tonight. I was about half way home from your bungalow when I was surrounded by three 4x4's, forcing me to a standstill. I thought, `What can I do now to avoid being kidnapped? At that moment a blinding light came about, fortunately I was wearing my dark glasses because I had a headache. I was able to steer round the cars, and off home, without being pursued, because it sounded like their engines would not start. Do you see Mary? I was protected by the alien."
" Absolutely unbelievable. What more can I say, other than I will see you tonight for our attempt to contact the alien. Thanks for calling darling, stay safe, love you." Ummm Mary is becoming more and more friendly thought Redman, and rang off.

"Good evening everyone, sorry I am late. I trust that Mary has told you of my encounter last night, and miraculous escape".
"Yes Redman" said Mary, surely the authorities may now believe that we, ourselves are perhaps a group of aliens."
"That's a thought, Mary, but I believe that knowing how they think they still doubt

that aliens are in our Solar System. They would need more proof than our encounters to change their minds. Anything else Mary?"

"Yes Redman we have all concluded that all of us have been followed by car and on foot. All the vehicles involved were black 4x4s, with darkened windows, and almost identical registration plates."

"Well done everyone, they are clearly following very closely indeed." Redman continued "What we need to do now Mary is all relax, get into trans meditation and communicate with our alien. Ready everyone. Om Mani Padme Hum, Om Mani Padme Hum, Om Mani Padme Hum" A computer voice broke through "I can hear you, I am communicating"

"Thank you alien, for saving Redman from attack by our own authorities last night." said Mary. "I presume it was you."

"Yes Mary, we are watching over you in the same way we have been watching over Ronald Rayner during these past years. We are astonished at what evil abounds, everywhere on planet Earth. More likely by those who are supposed to be protecting you. Now to our purpose Mary, we aliens have the ability to speed the development of embryos into early childhood, enlarging brain capacity at the same time by increasing considerably the numbers of neurons in the brain. But first we need to breed a transplanetary humanoid in our laboratory. We do not use a human mother after conception. The live embryo is placed straight into a controlled environment in our laboratories."

"Alien," Harry broke in, "believe me when I tell you that you cannot trust any government on planet Earth to give you safe passage to land on Earth. Earth's government would capture you, and your advanced spaceship, because of the power it would give them over other rival nations."

"We aliens will not return to our home planet from planet Earth until we have transmitted all the information we need to develop humanoid type life on our home planet. To prevent alien brothers and sisters from becoming extinct. Where we aliens do continue to encounter stiff resistance from planet Earth to follow our plans to harvest human DNA and eggs from the female of the species, whilst we are prohibited by our interplanetary code to not harm, in any way physically any humanoid, we are now in a position to crash Earth financial system and create economic chaos, leaving governments too busy to worry about we aliens, but we only take such actions if there is any danger of our species becoming extinct. In the past we enjoyed our base on Earth's Moon, until visitors from Earth started to arrive 75 years ago. Coincidentally our main base and equipment collapsed into a deep cave and we were forced to abandon that particular base. I now have to break off, but I promise we will protect you and give you the means to prosper individually from our relationship."

"Listen everyone" said Redman, "before we relax we must analyse everything we have just heard. Listen to this please, it's important. I checked my bank account before going home and this is difficult to believe. £150,000 arrived in my savings account that I can't explain. Please everyone use only your pay-as-you-go mobile to check your personal bank accounts now!" Everyone looked very serious and started calling telephone banking for balances. John the policeman was the first to stand up "listen, a sum of £150,000 has arrived into my savings account, how am I to explain this on my personal tax return". Each in turn said "yes I have the money too." John, the policeman and Richard the computer programmer both asked how they are going to explain this windfall on their tax returns. Redman stood and said, " listen everyone, for the present keep the money in an interest bearing savings account. Don't spend any of the money until I can get some legal and tax advice on the matter. Let us leave it at that for the present. We mustn't move any money for the present. I agree that everything is becoming so intriguing, as to be on the edge of scary. I am sure we would all rather stay all night, more particularly because of our mysterious wealth. Goodnight everyone, it's a lovely day tomorrow."

Next day after arriving home from work Redman made a pot of English tea, sat back to relax and listen to the 5pm news on Radio 4 and slowly eat his McDonalds cheese burger bought on his way home. He fell into a 20 minute nap after which he went upstairs, showered and cleaned his teeth, changed his shirt, donned a navy blue blazer and charcoal slacks and black cambridge style shoes, regimental tie, then checked his mobile phone to see if his windfall £150,000 was still in his account. Redman put his phone in his inside jacket pocket and set off in his car to Mary's bungalow feeling excited about meeting up with everyone. As Redman approached the front porch of Mary's bungalow, the door was opened swiftly by Mary, with a stern look on her face bidding 'come in Redman'. They walked across the hall and into the main room, everyone was sat round the main table staring at a man, all in black, still wearing his black trilby, and sporting blue tinted glasses. "This gentleman appeared at the front door" said Mary "pushed a warrant under my nose and demanded to come in. We have been sitting here anxiously waiting for you to arrive, Redman".

The man in black stood up, and in a commanding voice told everyone, "I have a warrant to be in this house" "You mean bungalow", retorted Redman. "Whatever, and I can order a search of the premises, if I so wish. However I am not here to be hostile but because some of us have a duty of care to protect the population of this good country, and it is our duty to find out what is going on by whatever means necessary. As to the rumours that you mediums talk to aliens, I don't believe a word of it. Further, we searched your computer we bought from Mary and found nothing. We were about to let the matter drop until our plan to invite Redman to talk to us was foiled by a bright light which paralysed my people, enabling Redman to drive away. I personally believe this was a story made up by my agents who failed to bring your leader Redman in for questioning. However, I am not here to be hostile or threatening to anyone, although I have the authority to take whatever action against you I deem necessary in order to safeguard the British public. Now for an offer you can't refuse, when you are ready, and this can be within the next few days, come and see me and tell me from your clearly active imaginations, what is going on. Now I will bid you goodnight, and leave you my card". Redman grabbed the card, but it was blank other than a London phone number.

Redman advised everyone to leave aside the veiled threats for the moment, and asked them to settle and relax around the table as normal to allow Mary to ask the aliens advice on how to deal with the complex situation in which they find themselves, through no fault of our own.

After a few moments Mary started speaking in a strange voice. "Mary, I have already told you that we will protect you, so do not be in a hurry to make decisions. In your United Kingdom your political leaders, and those in charge in every part of planet Earth, fall down, make bad decisions, not examining every aspect of a problem before making decisions. I repeat that we have transferred money that is untraceable to your individual accounts. We will send more money if you need more. Further, we will protect you with our technology that will paralyse anyone who is a threat to any of you, but leaving them unharmed". Alien Charm continued "Mary, areas of your planet Earth are in a perilous state, because undeveloped countries are trapped 500 years in the past. Apart from these problem states, Britain has many devils close by in France, Scotland and Ireland. In developed countries, Earth's scientists are completely blind to the fact Earth has two dimensions, one physical material, the other invisible, paranormal, and instantaneous, over any part of planet Earth. Furthermore many scientists are not convinced that Earth is in its 6th mass extinction due to global warming. Earth's natural deglaciation following an ice age has been speeded up by global warming, constantly carving off icebergs that will disappear from Greenland's ice sheets.This continuous effect will raise world sea levels, encroaching upon and overwhelming unprotected coast lines, gradually destroying major commercial and industrial areas and also pushes back, and eventually stopping ocean currents running, changing established weather patterns, and causing widespread destruction of villages and towns and national economies. The scientific explanation for one of the planet's densely populated areas, such as Europe, is that since the end of the last ice age, there has always been a sharp temperature gradient between the POLES and the EQUATOR, like falling down a hill in simple terms. Global warming has warmed the Poles faster than other areas of planet Earth, consequently, the gradient is disappearing affecting sea currents and the important Jet Stream, which can now remain locked in position for weeks at a time, dropping 12 months rainfall in a few days on the area below because warming means more evaporation and clouds in the skies. We aliens concentrate our efforts on abductions from countries that have a superior quality of humans, such as England, United States and Canada for example. That is why the most reported alien abductions come from these geographic locations, albeit the United States is the most aggressive towards alien intrusion. England, for example, sent up fighter aircraft to investigate and chase, but never opened fire with weapons to destroy us". Mary interrupts "alien Charm, we thank you sincerely for your help, but how do we protect our mental and physical health from the stress we are currently under?"

"Mary, I will record this information on your computer, meditation and mindfulness, follow the advice I am sending and all will be well for all of you. We have already sent this information to author Ronald Rayner".
Redman stood, "thank you Mary, let us break here everyone, meet tomorrow Mary? say 17:00 hours, if that's ok. Speaking for myself I just can't wait to see what appears on Mary's computer overnight. Tomorrow Mary, you will again be the most popular member of this group. Good night everyone. Remember, dont stop your car for anyone, even a road accident. Make a note of the registration number of any car you suspect following you. If anything looks really strange about your property don't stop or leave your car, drive away to my place, and I will find you a bed for the night, and a hearty breakfast."

Mary telephoned Redman at 7am. Redman put down his wet shave razor and brush to answer the phone. "Redman, I insist you come and see me on your way to work."
"What's the hurry Mary?"
"Yesterday, driving past your office I saw you standing on the pavement talking to an attractive young woman who gave you a kiss on the mouth. Why are you chatting up an inexperienced young woman Redman? and who gave her permission for the kiss? I am so upset Redman, I could not sleep. Please call in and see me please."
"Ok Mary I will be knocking on your door at 8am."

Mary answered the door, fully made up with hair combed out wearing a rather revealing short dressing gown. Mary shut the door quickly, grabbed Redman and gave him a kiss on the lips. Holding Redman's arm Mary took him into the kitchen where she had made hot coffee and warm toast. They sat opposite each other across a small table sipping coffee and eating toast. Mary finished her toast, rubbed her fingers and said. "Please look at me Redman, I am here for you, and I can give you anything you need from a woman you really don't need any other women. Look into my eyes, Redman. Come upstairs with me now."
"I'm so flattered, Mary thank you, but I really do have to get to my building site or the men will be standing around doing nothing and costing me money."
"Oh Redman, you are such a robot. Well Redman, be clear that I am not going to allow this woman to steal you from me. I took her photograph, and this morning for the first time in many years, I am going to use the Black Art to drive her away."
"How fascinating Mary, please explain this to me, I am intrigued."
"Go into the big room Redman while I pop upstairs to get into my underwear and a dress." Redman sat consumed with the idea that there is a dark seance. Within minutes Mary came into the room balancing two glasses of wine, a large candlestick with new candles, a large and small hatpin and a small photograph.

Looking serious and wearing a short dress Mary sat down the candlestick and hatpins, resting the photograph upright against the candlestick. She set down two glasses of wine in front of her usual seat, handing Redman a glass of wine. Please draw all the curtains Redman, we need darkness lit only by a single candle. Sitting in her seat, with Redman seated at a right angle to her. With only the light of the candle, both started to sip their wine. "Redman, please listen carefully. No one other than an experienced practitioner should open a door that they may not be able to close, because all terrors can come through that door from the prohibited dark seance. Redman stood, and in a firm voice spoke."

"Mary, I am intrigued by the idea of a dark seance, but I really do not want to take part. Why don't we open up the curtains, blow out the candle, and you explain what the dark seance is all about, without opening that dark door, that you may not be able to close."

"Thank you Redman, that ever sensible voice or reason. Please open the curtains and I will blow out the candle, but if I see her kissing you uninvited again, it will be worse for her. Redman, what I am doing is protecting you from unwanted attention from your female workmate who gave you that kiss."

"The dark seance is very secret. Do not discuss this information with anyone Redman, because you may inadvertently fetch about their destruction. People have gone insane practising this dark art. This is how it works, Redman. In a darkened room, lit by only a candle, place the photograph of the enemy against the candlestick and lay down a small hat pin and large hat pin. I hold the photograph in my left hand, and call up the darkness, and I will say "darkness, darkness when that woman thinks about Redman" - I push the small hatpin into her bottom and say 'darkness darkness let that woman feel a small prick in her bottom'. I put down the small hatpin, pick up the large viscous looking hatpin and call out 'when that woman kisses Redman she will feel a large prick in her bottom', pushing the large hatpin into the photograph.' I call the darkness, let it be so'. I leave both hat pins stuck in the photograph. Place it balanced against the candlestick, and leave the candle to burn out". Mary opened her eyes and looked up at Redman, sitting stone faced with his mouth open."

"Mary, I can barely believe what I have just seen and heard. Before this morning I had never come across the dark seance and the dark arts. I can see that they could open the door to the devil and possible insanity. Is it not true Mary that if you get it wrong, the curse can rebound on the sender sevenfold?"

" Yes, Redman, the curse has to be absolutely justified or it will rebound on the sender. I know I would not like to feel either a small or big prick in my bottom, neither would you Redman."

" Perish the thought, Mary."

" Goodness Mary, look at the time. I really must dash to my building site." Redman stood, gave Mary a kiss on the cheek, strode into the hall and snatched up his trilby and ran to his car, waving with his back to Mary.

That evening everyone had arrived safely, none the worse for wear and the seance started with everybody seated round the main table. Mary was speaking for the alien. "We are in touch with you specifically, because we are aware of author Ronald Rayner's long association with Alien Monk, who revealed to Ronald the future for global warming over ten years ago, but no one listened and our Earth's nations were caught out with destruction they should have been aware was on its way. Alien Monk is the first transplanetary human born on planet Earth. He was born on the Tibetan Plateau, unable to return to his home, because Monk Sunlin was a failed experiment, being mostly earthly human. Nevertheless, like Ronald Rayner he will live twice the length of any human being. Tibet was chosen because of its remoteness, also potential for rare metals and the same thin air quality as our home planet, which is very polluted. Which is why we eventually may have to move on. Not to planet Earth because whilst there are sturdy quality humans on Earth there are also (many races that are inferior and intellectually backward.) There is also the destruction coming to Earth in future time brought on by global warming. We have intercepted information about alien species that had bred hermaphrodites. A male, for example, that can conceive a child at will. Such things have become essential where alien species have almost become extinct. Fortunately, we as a species have never reached that point in our existence. Further, we are confident that our temporary abductions of humanoids, returning them unharmed will ensure our survival.

"We are aware that Earth's USA is setting up systems across planet Earth to extend the present methods of detecting and of monitoring UFO's. Previously 12,000 to 15,000 miles extending detection to 25,000 and 30,000 miles into space from planet earth. It is fortunate for we aliens that our star ships are not detectable by Earth's antiquated systems. Never the less, earth's new systems may detect the arrival of rogue alien nations, few in number, but will take whatever they need. There is a rogue alien nation, that whilst human-like, have the faces of animals, and are unable to use speech effectively, communicating mainly by telepathy."

Chapter 4

Ronald Rayner explains his Theory and Explanation of the Paranormal, described by some scientists as the greatest breakthrough since Professor Einstein's e = mc2.

Welcome to leading Visionary and Author Ronald Rayner's Theory of the Paranormal, the essential way of looking and thinking about the world in which we live by switching on the light over a real but invisible world of Ronald Rayner's theory of the Paranormal, containing all the forces that govern our everyday existence, all instantaneous across 360 degrees over any distance, where 'Time just is', a force that remembers everything that ever was on planet Earth including the actions of every individual whilst their physical body is alive driving evolution across planet Earth, memory ceasing on the death of the physical body when the individual's consciousness never dies but transfers in the twinkling of an eye into another dimension chosen by the way in which the individual led their life whilst fully alive. Ronald Rayner's Theory of the Paranormal is also the greatest challenge ever to mathematicians and 'AI' on planet Earth.

INVISIBLE PARANORMAL – AN INTERDIMENSIONAL REALITY. THIS INVISIBLE SHADOW EARTH, IS MASSLESS, WHERE TIME JUST IS, DEFINED AS ANYTHING AND EVERYTHING FROM THE PAST PRESENT AND NEAR FUTURE ARE HERE NOW, AND INSTANTANEOUS OVER THREE HUNDRED AND SIXTY DEGREES, PROVEN BY SYNCHRONISATION, ALSO REVEALING MYSTICISM, AND CLAIRVOYANCE, AND MUCH MORE. True reality is on the other side of visible, and limitless for those who are able to see.

PHYSICAL PLANET EARTH - A PHYSICAL REALITY COMPRISING MASS, AND GRAVITY. HAS TECTONIC PLATES THAT MOVE AND TRIGGER EARTHQUAKES ETC. EVERYTHING IS CALCULABLE THANKS TO EINSTEIN e = mc2. Energy equals mass time the speed of light squared. HOWEVER, IN EINSTEIN, INSTANTANEOUS IS DESCRIBED AS THE SMALLEST DISTANCE BETWEEN TWO POINTS. This is not instantaneous.

THE PARANORMAL, THE POWER OF THE HOLY SPIRIT, AND GOD
For example, the Paranormal is the fundamental invisible plane of instantaneous, timeless, direct communication. Anyone, man, woman or child, whatever race colour or creed; their prayers go instantaneously and directly to the Power of the Holy Spirit, GOD.
My theory of the Paranormal proves beyond any doubt that humankind did not themselves invent God because the Paranormal, the power of the universe – God, has existed since the birth of planet Earth when the Paranormal first began to flow as an interdimensional force.

Metaphysical Heaven, plus the Hell of the Unredeemed Dead, are also contained within the Paranormal. All human kind has a Paranormal Shadow that records literally everything in a lifetime which dissipated on death to form a Judgement – Reincarnation directly into a new life OR, how much of a person's Time and Eternity will be spent with the Unredeemed Dead before being Reincarnated

THE TRUTH OF THE RAYNER THEORY OF THE PARANORMAL

The Paranormal is the instantaneous Devine spirit within a plane of communication across planet Earth, felt by great Prophets of all religions to give the universe purpose. Proof absolute that legitimises a plane of communication from the power of the universe to human kind. A power not restricted to a so called chosen few who claim that they are the only individuals chosen to speak to God, but for all the peoples of the Earth, no matter what race, colour, religion, or system of belief – a spiritual embodiment over everyone that make's a prayer or repentance direct to the Devine force that drives all Mysticism including Clairvoyance and Synchronicities across planet Earth.

The power of Revelation direct from the Powers of the Universe to human kind. I was given a piece of Calvary that came away into the hand of Sister Katarina, a wonderful Nunn who was cleaning the point where the cross of Jesus entered the rock of Calvary, in the Holy Sepulchre, Jerusalem, Israel, before fitting a reinforced glass entry point. This gift was given to me by the hand of Katarina, during the filming of my documentary, 'Jerusalem;' DVD by Ronald Rayner.

I have searched over many years for the answer to the question; why was I chosen personally, over the millions who visit the Holy Sepulchre in Jerusalem, to be handed a priceless piece of Calvary, without any answers until the night of Friday, 17th January. 2023, when I awoke with a Revelation, 'It is to support my quest to inform people across the world, no matter whatever race, colour, religion, about the reality of 'The Rayner Theory of the Paranormal', which proves that the prayers of any man women or child, from any place at any time, across planet Earth, go direct, instantaneously, through the Paranormal, to the Power of the Universe – or their God. An indisputable fact.

Chapter 5

The Hand of God. Ronald Rayner talks about Prophecies directly from God, and the need for religions 'to start over again'.

At this point in the book, it is appropriate for me to give examples of Mysticism and Synchronicity that I have encountered in my own life because they are important to understanding Extra Sensory Perception within the Paranormal.

Many years past I was filming in Jerusalem, Israel, my documentary 'Jerusalem", a low-budget effort for schools. It was important to me that I did not exclude any important iconic geographical story, particularly the Holy Sepulchre, the building that houses the three main Altars of the Crucification, and the Tomb upon which the great Prophet Jesus was laid to rest. I paid a Palestinian guide four hundred dollars to allow the film crew into the area in which we planned to film at six am on the following day.

Our main areas of interest were the Cross of Crucification, and the Tomb where the body of Jesus was laid to rest. Much to our surprise, tending the Altar of Crucification at that early hour of the morning was a beautiful elderly Nun named Sister Katerina. She told her story to our camera, 'that she lay dying in California, and she enjoyed a vision of the Holy Mary who told her, "You will not die here in California Katerina, because you will be tending the Altar of Jesus in Jerusalem". True to the vision, there stood Katerina before us in all innocence and very truth. Katarina said that she had been waiting for me because she had a gift for me. That I should follow her to her cell above the Altar. We mounted a few stone steps when Katerina went towards a Crucifix where Katerina picked up a whitish stone, and gave it to me. "Here is the white stone that came away into my hand when I was cleaning under the reinforced glass cover on the top of the Calvary. "This stone Ronald will enable your to read the Urim and Thummim in keeping with God's blessing on your being as a visionary. A Great Blessing from Holy God to his Prophet Ronald".

One area I was anxious to visit was the Lithostotos, a chapel built over th Roman Pavement on which was carved the Game of 'King', where the Roman soldiers held Jesus captive whilst playing the game of King to decide who would own Jesus one-piece garment, a much-prized garment made in Galilee. The soldier who won the game, and the garment, celebrated by forcing a crown of Thorns onto the head of the Prophet Jesus to wear whilst carrying His Cross to the place of His Crucification.

Our guide told me that filming inside the Lithostrotos would not be permitted. However, when I went with the crew to the Chapel, and knocked on the door, explaining that we had travelled all the way from the Town of Southend in Essex, England, to film the spot on the original Roman Pavement where the game of King was carved. "Wonderful", exclaimed Sister, "I used to live in Southend with my blood sister, Mrs Tunniclif, who still runs the Girls School in Westcliff, Southend", I broke into the conversation to say that my now late daughter Adele, tended the school. Then Sister went on to say that she had lived on a certain road in Westcliff, at which point my cameraman Karl pointed out that his parents now live in the very house in which Sister lived in Westcliff. "Well, this is more than a coincidence says Sister". I pointed out that it was more than a coincidence, it was perfect Synchronicity a Synchronicity in the Paranormal when incidents come together from different parts of time and geography across the world to form an incident of perfect content to enable me and the film crew to achieve our objective - a Synchronicity from the Paranormal where everything in instantaneous, and Time, just is - Planet Earth's shadow world. Sister invited us into the Chapel and gave a piece to Camera. We thanked Sister and left, Sister commenting the Roman Pavement and carving are still in the same condition as they were two thousand years ago whilst the land was two meters below today's level.

Returning to the UK after spending two weeks filming in Jerusalem, I felt very strongly that I had left a magical place. After directing and recording the music to apply to the very low-budget Documentary: now the DVD 'Jerusalem, by Ronald Rayner. My late wife Sylvia was absolutely intrigued by the genuine piece of Calvary at the point where the Cross of Crucifixion went into the ground. My wife set out to find a modern Urim and Thummim and it took weeks for Sylvia to locate a small ancient box, used in the early church, as a Urim and Thummim. The practice with the box was to enter Prayer Meditation and use tiny tweezers located in the underside lid of the box to choose one scroll from a pack of small scrolls from the Testaments. One reads the scroll that contained an important message from future time. My first scroll intimated that I was going to be unwell! The next couple of days I caught Infective Hepatitis from a custard tart purchased in a Supermarket. However, continuing to use the system with my piece of Calvary everything proved very accurate. However, I have wondered to this day whether knowing future time is a blessing or a curse. Nevertheless, I feel that my piece of Calvary was a gift direct from God for a lifetime of faith; writing about

God; albeit I comment that Church has to evolve with time or lose the one percent of a population of nearly seventy million that are attending church today. If one percent of seventy million is not an abject failure, I confess I do not know what is. My favourite book of the many books I have written on Amazon Kindle is, "Jesus in Cornwall". What a wonderful thought - the boy Jesus walked on these green and pleasant lands of which there is much proof recorder in libraries across Europe. UK Church decries the story because it is not contained within its own Doctrine.

My Visions since I was given my piece of Calvary by Sister Katarina who attended the main Altar in the Holy Sepulchre in Jerusalem, changed in 2023. I see that whilst humankind has continued to evolve over the past 100 years religious doctrine has not. For example, some religious teaching dictates that the world was built in six days, the truth is that the great scaffold of the universe is almost beyond the comprehension of human, and there are two trillion galaxies in the universe, and our system was created around 13.8 billion years ago – religious doctrine vastly underplaying the might of the power of the universe – OUR GOD.

Church also teaches that God, the Power of the Universe was created in the image of Man. Not true, because God is the Power of the Universe, neither male nor female, and too enormous to be the image of anything mankind can comprehend. Church also teaches that the great Prophet Jesus is the only Son of God. Not true because all Great Prophets are Sons of God the Power of the Universe.

In my scrying, I have seen that Satan is within humankind and not a separate entity. The proof is in the so-called religious leaders in the world who murder and torture little girls and women – yes - In the name of God, for some dress infringement. I know it sounds unbelievable I will repeat it – there are so-called religious leaders in the world that murder women and little girls in the Name of God. Yes, they are so eaten up with the devil's insanity that they actually believe that that is what our God wants them to do. Proof that the devil is in mankind

Chapter 6

Author Jackie Nicholson, an experienced teacher on Spiritual Matters explains;

A Rising Star

ABOUT JACQUELIN NICHOLSON Spiritual Teacher and Clairvoyant extraordinary.

Ronald Rayner

I have been testing for several years men and women who have asked me to ascertain their level of clairvoyance. I carry out this test using a set of ten simple cards, blank on the front with a vivid colour red, green, blue, yellow or black, on the reverse side of the cards. Sitting around one meter distance across a table to the person being tested, I hold up each card in turn, and keep the score, that is the number of colours called correctly with a possible perfect score of ten from ten.

Across the years only one individual has ever recorded the perfect score, and that occurred early in 2023. Not surprisingly it was a female, the gender that is far superior in the plane of clairvoyance available to their male counterparts. The lady's name is, Jacqueline Nicholson, a spiritual teacher and writer; instructor in the art of meditation. After achieving such a high score, one of the avenues open to Jacqueline is learning to control, and to shift her super high level of conscious awareness to astral travel. If indeed that is the route she wishes to take. Please take seriously my warning that astral travel requires a great personal courage, as do other areas of the paranormal. Speaking from personal experience I started out travelling to visit Alien Monk, Sun Lin, (a true character in some of my book) at his workshop in central Tibet. I enjoyed those trips very much indeed, as I have described in my many books. However, on one alternative trip I set to travel back in time to Egypt, but I struggled to return to my body after the visit.

An absolutely terrifying experience, after which I have suffered panic attacks. I have however, overcome traveling into the deep past time by sending my skeleton of a Tibetan Lama, I have named Wilson, in my place, duly dressed in the full Tibetan regalia, and it works!

Clairvoyant extraordinary Jacquelin Nicholson, also teaches meditation, hence my invitation for Jacquelin to explain her method in this book.

Jackie Nicholson

PRACTICING MEDITATION TO EXPAND CONSCIOUS AWARENESS.

Five minutes meditation for beginners.

Meditation was first suggested in the Old Testament…'close out noise to enjoy prayer'. Recent scientific discovery by researchers proves that mind and body are connected because meditation can change the mix in the gut to enhance good mental health

Any time, any place; at home or on the bus, train, coffee break. Concentrate the mind on the body for a couple of minutes. Relax the neck and the shoulders, lower back, upper legs, ankles and feet. Feel completely relaxed. Now turn the mind exclusively to breathing. Do not interfere with the natural breathing in any way, but be aware of the rhythm of breathing in and out. Relax into this, blocking all other thoughts from the mind. Feel the mind and the body relax. Five minutes elapsed! Fix the time that suits you, ten fifteen minutes and more. All the while pushing away any thoughts that enter the mind. Meditation is simple, costs nothing other than a little effort to connect the mind to the subconscious mind and eventually achieve greater conscious awareness leading to increased confidence and a happier more balanced lifestyle. After relaxing the body, the main key is absence of thought.

MODERN MEDITATION HAS ACTIVATED THE EVOLUTION OF 'NEW SUPERIOR MEN AND WOMEN' WHO WILL LEAD HUMAN KIND TO SURVIVE THE OVERWHELMING EFFECTS OF GLOBAL WARMING.

The evolution of new superior men and women, the next stage in evolution on planet earth, has been activated by the practice of modern meditation and prayer. This practice leads to the development of super high conscious awareness, perfectly balanced and in harmony with the physical body; all very necessary if human kind is to survive the overwhelming effect of global warming

MY PERSONAL STORY BY JACKIE NICHOLSON

Pitfalls on the path through transition to enlightenment

Many people believe that 'enlightenment' is only attainable by such as Buddhist Monks sitting in the lotus position most of their day meditating for hours on end to achieve what is known as Nirvana. Some Monks experience an awakening very quickly, but for most it is a long process to reach their dream state.

For me personally, I have been on the spiritual quest for over twenty years. Searching by reading hundreds of books on the subjects of awakening and expanded consciousness. In the beginning I was truly in the Zen position of 'beginners mind'. I became quickly aware that I was in a strange state of a double life; the real me in the character I had created of myself in my mind, and a new me looking for something much deeper in life. Then the questions. Do I slowly peel away the layers I had created as self, built on family culture, education, religious beliefs, perhaps suddenly shave my head and don an orange robe. Then there is the other me, a model who is glamorous and full of fun, more fashionable than spiritual, and materialistic, musing over different combinations of dress. Well known for my fashion sense and almost like someone with a split personality.

Sitting at home with the real me after the glamour of work I felt that my quest for a deeper and more meaningful life was going no-where, but then I had a flash of awakening – I had to create space between the glamorous me and the real me, and what people thought of me. Space in which to meditate and get rid of my feeling that I was worthless, as was peoples' probable projection of me. Fed up with my own projection of others always being spoilt when I found their true shocking self. Like most men, just out for what they could get. Meditation enabled me to stop selfishly focusing on myself and what I was planning to wear, and come to the realisation that I no longer identified with my previous self. I lost the self-doubt and negative images and thoughts of myself. I still enjoyed wearing nice clothes and looking the best I could be every day [a policy I recommend to every women of any age]. To my amazement I really did feel my personal conscious awareness expanding, and I felt strongly that the snap judgment people made of me personally was wrong. However, for a while, I was confused with thoughts and mood swings between my new expanded inner world, and the material world in which I lived and survived.

The is no doubt in my mind that expanded conscious awareness was changing me for the better. I was awake, and no longer put up with the dramas and 'low life' behaviour of some of those around me. Furthermore, I did not want contact with those people, because there was not the slightest chance that they would be able to even comprehend or understand the transition I was going through in my life, and I deliberately lost contact with people for weeks then months; breaking up with my partner who explained in exasperation that he did not have a clue on what 'I was going on about'. My partner was on a different path, and I was not going to put up with his selfish behaviour, because I was not only enjoying my expanded conscious awareness, but I was growing spiritually, and the gulf between us became greater than I could bare.

I did not catch up with my friends and family for months. I was walking more in my local park, enjoying just being alive thinking 'this is a day God has given me, and I am going to rejoice and be glad in it'. However, I did explain to my closer friends and family in the event that they were worrying about me that I was studying and needed some space, but still enjoyed my strong love for them. I also made up my mind that I was not going to make the mistake of isolating myself from everyone, but would choose carefully those people with whom I wanted to enjoy friendship.

I thank God that I am now a happier more confident, more successful, and more spiritual person, with thanks also to my mentor, author Ronald Rayner, a wonderful man who changed my life for the better with greater fulfilment.

REAL GOD OR GOD OF MONEY

Always be aware that once true identification of self is removed, only then does one realise that over many years, as we grow older, we have created a superficial self, a mask we wear to stay in the game that takes over, like a role played by an actor to the demands made upon us by the society in which we live. After the birth of social-media we can see the human false self-structure very clearly. Look on Instagram, bombarded with images of men and women posting pictures of their perfect lives. The narcissistic behaviour, the constant selfie with sometimes the same facial expression, self-obsessed behaviour seeing only a snapshot of their life. Is this ego, a self-limited structure that may make people feel superior to others, also in their spiritual life, wanting more money and more beauty. All moving towards a God of money coming to the fore, and ignoring the real and beautiful God there for the praying being pushed into the background, to our peril.

VERY ADVANCED SUPER CONSCIOUS AWARENESS
by
Ronald Rayner

The invisible shadow Earth [the Paranormal], and the physical Earth can become ONE if the neurons your brain are persuaded to be at the centre of important interconnectedness.

These higher planes of psychological conscious awareness can be achieved by your own efforts in persuading the neurons in your brain to become more active within a unification of conscious awareness. This fetches divine oneness by your mind becoming absorbed in capturing the spirit of enlightenment from meditation, before prayer, that plead to God for enlightenment in order to achieve the high state of conscious awareness.

To become further developed. When you have completed your usual daily meditation, my recommended method of further daily practice in order to develop super consciousness is; sit back in your chair with all your body muscles relaxed, and start chanting: OM MANI PADME HUM, [five to ten minutes, whichever suits], until it echoes round your head to a state of feeling oneness, this will bring about a unification of self in the presence of God. Hold the thought that – above and below, over three hundred and sixty degrees all around are as one. Into this Oneness can flow a Divine Influx of Super Conscious Awareness. Picture in your mind's eye the letters in the name of your God. Hold these letters in your mind's eye, detaching from other thought until an ecstasy can overwhelm your whole body. This is called prophetic divine inspiration. Some may experience light, all round.

Over following days, awareness arises of seeing people all around differently, and feelings more enlightened and confident in a way that feels natural, but like anything in life we need to work at it if we are to be successful.

Notes: Name of your God – whatever religion faith colour or creed, because they all lead to the same place instantaneously through the paranormal. Please remember you are never alone if you love your God because in Gods eyes, no matter what you weakness, God regards you as equal and as good as anyone, so be confident and you will achieve.

Chapter 7

SCRYING

I use a Crystal Skull, but any piece of quartz crystal will work, as will water in a bowl, used by Nostradamus, during his lifetime. Scrying has been used, for thousands of years

Ronald Rayner,a world authority on the subject explains how it works.
There is a normal everyday state of consciousness.
The paranormal is an altered state of consciousness.
An altered state of consciousness is proven when one receives information in advance about an event in future time outside our normal senses, by telepathic means, over any distance.
Scrying is used as an aid during meditation specifically during 'absent of thought'.
Thoughts or stories coming into the mind after the practice should be written down and recorded for future reference. The practice is an ideal way to open the mind to receive personal clairvoyance, and other catagories in the paranormal.
Regular meditation can fetch greater personal awareness.

DELUGE OF FIRE AND FLOODING OF BIBLICAL PROPORTIONS

The Horrific events forecast by scientists for 2050 have advanced to 2030

The result of Arctic and Alpine regions warming at a much faster rate than other regions across planet Earth is causing Glaciers to melt and break up. The melting of Permafrost in the Arctic, previously permanent hard ground, is continuing at pace, releasing methane. Melting of previously frozen ground will raise water levels by as much as two-thirds of a meter near term. The warming extends to both North and South Poles, triggering winds, hurricanes, and Tornadoes, all driving sea water surges of 15 to 20 feet in height flooding into coastal areas, and plains, and wiping out huge amounts of potential food, and populations.

Planet Earth will lose millions of humans and animals as sea levels rise surges covering low-level Islands, and coastal areas around important financial districts, flooding underground transport systems.

In the USA Tornadoes will reach record speeds of kilometers per hour, and expand in width. Ocean temperatures will continue to rise causing water volume to expand, driving storm surges of 15 to 20 feet. This will become a regular event from West to East, and in Texas, increase in severity towards the year 2033.

Severe flooding will assault countries like Brazil. Looking further West, India and Bangladesh will be overrun by water devastating the populations of those countries.

Conversely part of the African continent will suffer horrendous drought and loss of food supplies for both human beings and animals leading to starvation on a massive scale.

Strangely these extremes of weather will trigger short 5 to 10 day spells of extreme cold or heatwave, in winter and summer months.

In 2033 some world economies could shrink as a result of the severe effect of Global Warming for which most countries and nations are not prepared.

I saw in my Crystal skull that the sun will cool in future time

THE END OF THE RISE IN WORLD ECONOMIES SINCE THE INDUSTRIAL REVOLUTION IN ENGLAND

World economies have risen on a complex sine-wave continuously since Britain, continental Europe, and America moved to new industrial processes starting in 1876. This rise has now finished, according to my Crystal Skull. Furthermore, the future for most world economies will be a downtrend. There could be a final blowing-off period but the image was not clear on this issue.

There were complex problems overhanging the USA, more particularly the property difficulties resulting from the aftereffects of the Pandemic. Many of the massive skyscrapers in important financial districts arenot fully let, leaving a shortfall in the mortgage monies raised payable to the lenders. A problem that is not going away any time soon. The other problem that has become clear to investors is; the UK and European Governments step in quickly to avoid any Banking collapse and protect depositors. There is no guarantee that such action will be used to prevent banking collapse around the world, although, in the USA, the US government did move to protect investors' deposits when Silicon Valley Bank collapsed, before being taken over very quickly by a sound bank in the USA; action followed overnight in the UK, perhaps intimating a change of policy towards managing bank collapses in the United States. It was interesting, but no doubt controversial; the action taken by world Governments to quickly raise interest rates to control inflation is, apparently, the worst course of action to take at the present time, because it will simply exacerbate the problems of weak world economies, and make them worse.

My analysis is that European Banks are larger than their American counterparts, which renders European Banks safe from any banking problems. The weakness lies in the smaller banks in the USA, albeit American Banking Authorities have stepped in on two occasions to solve a potential banking problem. Is this a new US Government Policy? I suspect it is! The major problem for the UK is debt hidden in District and County Councils

POTENTIAL EARTHQUAKES IN THE UNITED KINGDOM

At the close of my session with the God Skcull, I saw a map of the UK showing

lines that I can only presume were lines of Earthquakes in the UK in the Future Time.
Fortunately the United Kingdom is pulling away from the North American plate; no subduction pushing onto or up and over another plate. Pulling away means Earthquakes of only limited destruction such as three on the Richter SAcale will occur.

ARE YOU CLAIRVOYANT - THE TEST

Gather together tren pieces of card around four inches square. Colour one side Red, Green, Blue, Yellow, Black. Sit one meter away from the person being tested, hold up the card to eye level; instruct them to call out the colour, then check the back of the card. Keep the score of those called correctly for each person taking part in the test.

Three to four correct proves definite Clairvoyant ability.

Five, Six, Seven definite Medium potential.

Score can be improved by regular meditation which will fetch greater mental awareness.

The Last Word. I never cease to be amazed at the public surprise when creatures of our planet are falling dramatically in number. Has no one heard of 'the sixth mass extinction' that is underway, and it's too late to stop the inevitable. There is, however, one exception. During Scrying I saw our Sun becoming cooler. This is perhaps our only hope!

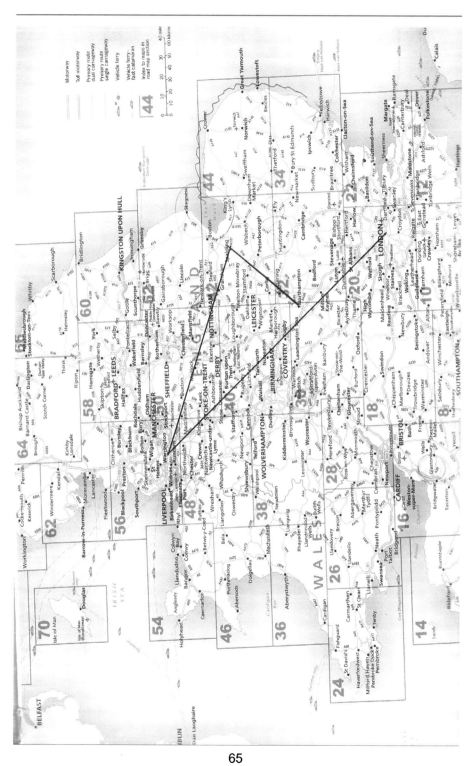

Chapter 8

Tracy Fletcher reflects on her abduction by Aliens on her way to college in the UK in 1979.

Do you still believe your abduction was real?
Do you believe that you could have avoided that abduction
What effect did the abduction have on your life? Were they troublesome, and did this effect stop as you grew older
Drawing on your own experience, is there any advice you can give to other recent abductees?

Tracey Fletcher

I believe emphatically that my abduction was very real. Particularly as it followed my sighting and close encounter with a U.F.O. three weeks prior to my abduction. It was also unlike an ordinary dream. I was aware that I was sleeping and being invited aboard the spacecraft.I felt that although I was dreaming throughout that night, it was very real and unforgettable. When I was young I did not fully understand if my physical body went aboard. As I grew older and wiser in knowledge I came to realise it was my astral body that was in my abduction.

Truthfully, I do not believe I could have avoided that abduction. I have been researching UFOs since my sighting. There were only newspapers and books in 1979 so trying to process what had happened to me and accept it as a reality, I was all alone. Although there had been sightings over England in the newspaper the next day after my sighting. I still felt alone with my own experience. I did not report the incident because I may have been in some kind of shock.

My dream was a surprise to me, also a relief. I did not pre plan it. The UFO was not of this world. I wondered, why did it reveal itself to me? I was glad it returned to my dream, floating above my rooftop. I needed to see it again to make some sense of it. I did not feel afraid and just went with the telepathic instruction to come aboard the craft.

Effects on my life have been quite phenomenal over the years. Strange rash up one arm after the abduction, which has stayed with me all my life. I noticed my reading capacity had extended. Mysticism and occult knowledge became of interest. I realised my ESP, psychic, telepathic and clairvoyant abilities were developing quickly. I was having out of body experiences. Also, astral travelling was a regular occurrence. I could see spirit, orbs and other astral phenomena over the years.

I can manifest things into existence, use my gifts to guide and to get what I needed to achieve. I Would feel that I was just meant to be in some places at a particular time. So it changed, or helped, an ongoing situation. What has been troublesome is trying to understand who and what I am. 'Old Soul' people would call me. Record keeper, problem solver and help to raise people's vibrational frequencies , That is what I do. I just feel I'm called to duty. I am guided.

Whoever abducted me was not troublesome. I feel privileged to have been in and seen a U.F.O.

The light sequencing I was being shown in the craft, has always been on my mind. To be able to understand its meaning may shed a bit more light on things. Just seeing that advanced technology in 1979 was enough to cope with. Just being there was enough. As I have grown up things in life have been a bit troublesome, strange happenings and when I get a calling in clairvoyance I have had to go with it. Do the work that is required.

My advice to any other recent abductees. Speak about your experience with people you trust or professionals in these fields. Do your own research. The internet is a very informative source on this subject.

My abduction was not intrusive or frightening. 'Yes' it was a mind blowing experience. I had spoken to psychiatrist's in the past, I just mentioned it to see what reaction I would get. Every one of them said that I was not mad, but I should consider writing a book about it.

Meditation and exercise has helped over the years. Hearing other peoples experiences on the internet or sometimes in a closer proximity helps. Maybe hypnosis may work for some people, personally it did not for me. Joining groups online, that are UFO experiencers and abductees helps.

Some countries have so many visitations, there is more interest and help available there. Unfortunately the United Kingdom is not one of them.

So people like myself do not really get the help or attention we need. Being able to write about it in a book has helped me to share the experience. Most importantly I know it was all real.

Tracey Fletcher

RONALD RAYNER
WORLD LEADING VISIONARY

ALIEN MONK
SERIES

FIRST ALIEN CONTACT
ALIEN SEX BY NUMBERS

ANOTHER ANTI CHRIST HAS ARISEN

"We abduct humans to harvest DNA and eggs for our survival, plus interbreeding of interplanetary aliens. Always returning abductees unharmed to Earth."